THE HAZY MOON
OF ENLIGHTENMENT

THE HAZY MOON

MOON

of ENLIGHTENMENT

HAKUYU TAIZAN MAEZUMI
AND BERNIE GLASSMAN

FOREWORD BY CHÖGYAM TRUNGPA RINPOCHE

PREFACE BY BERNIE GLASSMAN

REVISED AND EXPANDED EDITION

EDITED BY WENDY EGYOKU NAKAO
AND JOHN DAISHIN BUKSBAZEN

WISDOM PUBLICATIONS • BOSTON

Wisdom Publications
199 Elm Street
Somerville MA 02144 USA
www.wisdompubs.org

The Appendix by Neal Donner is reprinted with permission from *The Ten Directions* (Volume II, number 3): Zen Center of Los Angeles and the Institute for Transcultural Studies, Los Angeles.

Library of Congress Cataloging-in-Publication Data
Maezumi, Hakuyu Taizan.
  The hazy moon of enlightenment : part of the on Zen practice series / Hakuyu Taizan Maezumi and Bernie Glassman ; foreword by Chögyam Trungpa Rinpoche ; preface by Bernie Glassman. — Rev. and expanded ed. / Wendy Egyoku Nakao and John Daishin Buksbazen.
     p. cm.
  Includes bibliographical references and index.
  ISBN 0-86171-314-1 (pbk. : alk. paper)
  1. Spiritual life—Zen Buddhism. 2. Enlightenment (Zen Buddhism) I. Glassman, Bernard (Bernard Tetsugen) II. Nakao, Wendy Egyoku. III. Buksbazen, John Daishin, 1939- IV. Title.
  BQ9288.M332 2007
  294.3'444—dc22
                          2006033575

ISBN 0-86171-314-1

First Wisdom edition
11 10 09 08 07
5   4   3   2   1

Cover designed by TLrggms. Interior designed by Gopa&Ted2, Inc. Set in Aldus 10.5/14.

Printed in the United States of America

Though clear waters range to the vast blue autumn sky,

How can they compare with the hazy moon on a spring night!

Most people want to have pure clarity,

But sweep as you will, you cannot empty the mind.

—Keizan Zenji

Contents

Foreword to the First Edition

IT IS A PRIVILEGE to write this foreword, which seems to mark a joining of the clarity of Zen tradition with the vividness of Tibetan tradition. In the United States, Zen has been the vanguard of Buddhadharma, and it remains genuine and powerful. Its simplicity and uncompromising style have caused Western minds to shed their complexities and confused ideology. It has been remarkable to see Western students of Zen giving up their territory of ego purely by sitting, which is the genuine style of Shakyamuni Buddha. On the other hand, some people tend to glamorize their ego by appreciating Zen as a coffee table object or by dabbling in Zen rhetoric. Another problem has been fascination with cultural beauty, causing a failure to appreciate the austerity of the true practicing tradition.

As we know, the word *zen* derives from the Chinese word *chan,* from the Sanskrit *dhyana,* meaning "meditation." In Tibetan, it is *samten.* *Sam* means "cognitive mind" and *ten* means "steady." So samten, or Zen, is the notion of being in a state of stillness. In the Dasabhumika Sutra and the Samadhiraja Sutra, the Buddha talks about the means for practicing dhyana as cultivating the right motive, which is refraining from fascination with external sensory input. This technique has become one of the most powerful in overcoming fundamental dualism between self and others, and to overcome psychological materialism. Psychological materialism is shielding oneself from the fear of death and decay through intellectual and aesthetic pursuits, trying to make oneself into a perfect work of art.

The most profound right motive, according to the Tathagatagarbha Sutra, is to awaken oneself to buddha nature. Whenever doubt arises, one should cut through it; doing this, one finds behind it a state of brilliant wakefulness. The doubt which must be cut through is not so much intellectual uncertainty, but general slothfulness.

There are the different traditions of sudden and gradual paths to realizing buddha nature. But it seems that the conclusion is the same, no matter how suddenly it dawns. Still, every path has a beginning, middle and end. Therefore sudden could be called gradual, and vice versa. As long as there is a need for clearing away clouds of confusion, there is a path. In fact, the concepts of sudden and gradual are merely mental flickers. In either case, when the student begins to have a longing or passion for buddha nature as his prize, that in itself is an obstacle. Sometimes we find that very dedicated students have difficulty in making progress. When there is some freedom combined with tremendous exertion and practice, then buddha nature begins to shine through. But it seems to be dangerous to talk too much about buddha nature: we might formulate a mental image of it.

When this twofold right motive of non-harming and of awakening begins to develop in the practitioner, then the sense of stillness begins to dawn. In this case, stillness is not something distinguished from motion; it is stillness without beginning or end. In this stillness, the five eyes of the buddha begin to open, so that finally dhyana gives birth to *prajna,* which is the sixth paramita of the bodhisattva path. Prajna, or discriminating awareness, is a two-edged sword which cuts oneself and others simultaneously. At the level of the emergence of prajna, the experience of *samadhi* becomes apparent. *Samadhi* means "being there" or "holding acutely." According to the sutras, there are millions of samadhis, but they all simplify into two approaches: *sugata,* which is "well-gone," and *tathagata,* "gone as it is." Both achieve the *tathata,* which is "as it is."

It is very soothing to talk about these things; however, if there is no exertion and wakefulness we are not even finger-painting, but deceiving ourselves in the name of the Dharma. I feel that the existence of the practice tradition is the only hope. It alone can wage war against ego. It alone is the way that we can comprehend the Dharma.

The Venerable Taizan Maezumi Roshi's teaching has caused true Zen to penetrate into people's minds and has cut through the trappings of their ego-oriented intentions. I have strong conviction that through his wisdom, Buddhadharma will shine into the world, dispelling the darkness of samsaric confusion and bringing the gentle rain of compassion.

Riding the horse of mirage
Watching the sea of stars
Blossoming great eastern sun.

Chögyam Trungpa
The Kalapa Camp
December 1977

Preface to the First Edition

THE THREE BOOKS in the "On Zen Practice" trilogy*—*On Zen Practice: Foundations of Practice, On Zen Practice II: Body, Breath, and Mind,* and *The Hazy Moon of Enlightenment*—reflect the teachings of Taizan Maezumi Roshi through three generations, and include talks by Maezumi Roshi himself, by his teachers and dharma dialogues with his disciple Bernie Tetsugen Glassman Sensei (who has since become Roshi Bernie Glassman). The trilogy, therefore, presents Zen practice as it existed in Japan, as it has existed in the transitional phase in which a Japanese Zen master presents it to an American audience, and as it is manifesting itself in its new environment, with American students teaching it in the American idiom.

Dogen Zenji, the founder of Japanese Soto Zen, describes practice as a spiral of four phases. The first is *raising the bodhi-mind,* raising the desire for enlightenment; in other words, vowing to ourselves and to others that we will accomplish the Way, attain the realization of who we are, together with all sentient beings. The second phase is *practice:* putting our full effort into these vows and giving them life by striving toward the accomplishment of the unaccomplishable. The third is *realization:* with strong vows and determination to accomplish the Way; this steady, consistent practice ultimately results in realization, understanding, insight. And the fourth is *nirvana:* letting go of what we have realized and renewing our vows to again accomplish the Way, practice,

---

*In 2002, the first two books of the trilogy were combined in one volume from Wisdom Publications titled *On Zen Practice: Body, Breath, Mind.*

realize, and let go. This spiral continues endlessly, increasing in depth and in breadth, encompassing all things.

On Zen Practice: Foundations of Practice, the first book in the trilogy, explores the fundamental questions we ask when we first give rise to an aspiration to practice: What is practice? Why practice? What is effort? What is sesshin? *On Zen Practice II: Body, Breath, and Mind*, goes on to describe aspects of Zen practice in detail and includes articles on koan practice and shikantaza, breathing, gassho and bowing, and receiving the precepts.

The present volume, *The Hazy Moon of Enlightenment*, presents the third and fourth phases of this endless spiral. Parts one and two, "Enlightenment" and "Delusion," tell what there is to realize—what enlightenment means, what delusion means, and why Dogen Zenji says that "enlightenment is delusion." The last part, "Enlightenment in Action," presents the active state of nirvana, the state of letting go and going on, as embodied in the Eight Awarenesses of the enlightened person. Both the book and the trilogy end at this point, but as Dogen Zenji also says, our practice is endless. In reality, the end of this book brings us back to the first volume, *On Zen Practice*, in which we again renew our vows and ask: *Why practice? Who am I?*

Another way of looking at our practice is revealed by examining the following koan: Master Shishuang Qingzhu (J. Sekiso Keisho) said, "How will you step from the top of a hundred-foot pole?"

Since we are always on top of a hundred-foot pole, the question here is, "Being where you are right now, how do you go one step further? What is at the end of that one step?" Taking that step, we realize what we are, what life is, but we again find ourselves on top of a hundred-foot pole, clinging desperately to the tip, not wanting to fall off and yet knowing we must go further. So again and again, we have to take that step and find out what's at the end of it. On top of the high mountain, we can see boundless mountains above. Reaching to the highest of them, still we can see boundless clouds heaped one on top of another, and beyond that the vast and empty sky endlessly expanding. Let's take those steps together and accomplish the Way with all beings.

—Bernie Glassman

Editors' Preface
to the Revised Edition

THIS EDITION of *The Hazy Moon of Enlightenment* has been revised and expanded. The original material, which consisted of *teisho* (formal Dharma talks) given by Maezumi Roshi and discussions led by Bernie Tetsugen Glassman Sensei, has been preserved with some editing for clarification and accessibility.

Two important additions to this edition of *The Hazy Moon of Enlightenment* are Neal Donner's essay on the sudden and gradual enlightenment schools of Chan Buddhism and Flora Eko Courtois' *Experience of Enlightenment*. Neal Donner's penetrating discussion of sudden and gradual enlightenment sheds light on the simplistic dualism of the Northern and Southern School debate.

The final section of this expanded edition is *An Experience of Enlightenment* by Flora Eko Courtois. This piece was originally published in a limited edition by Center Publications in the early 1970s and subsequently reissued by the Theosophical Publishing House in 1986. Upon her death in 2000, she left the copyright of her book to the Zen Center of Los Angeles. It had been her intention to update the Afterword, but she had not done this by the time of her death. This reissuing of her memoir fulfills our promise to her to republish this work.

It is with deep appreciation for her pioneering presence as one of the first American Zen students that we have the honor of republishing this first-person account of her awakening.

We wish to gratefully acknowledge the White Plum Sanghas, which includes the Dharma successors and practitioners in Maezumi Roshi's lineage, and especially the sangha of ZCLA/Buddha Essence Temple, for their encouragement and support of this project.

We wish to acknowledge the assistance rendered by Burt Wetanson and Kathy Isshin Havens in the preparation of this manuscript.

Our deep appreciation also to Josh Bartok, our editor and collaborator at Wisdom Publications, for his support of this project.

As editors of this volume and the beneficiaries of many years of Maezumi Roshi's teaching, we offer our efforts with profound gratitude to him. May the merits of these teachings reflect the wisdom and compassion of Maezumi Roshi, and whatever shortcomings our renderings may have be attributed solely to us.

Wendy Egyoku Nakao
John Daishin Buksbazen
Zen Center of Los Angeles
Buddha Essence Temple
June 2006

I. Enlightenment

1: The Sound of Enlightenment

Taizan Maezumi

THERE IS A FAMOUS HAIKU by the Japanese poet, Matsuo Basho (1644–1694):

> *Old pond,*
> *Frog jumps in—*
> *The sound of water.*

Not only was Basho a master of haiku, he also studied Zen under a priest by the name of Buccho, with whom he had a close friendship in addition to their teacher-student relationship. When he composed this famous haiku, he was living in Tokyo in a small hut. One day, after a brief rain, Buccho Zenji visited Basho, and as a greeting asked: "How's your understanding these days?" Basho responded, "Rain has passed; green moss moistened." Buccho Zenji probed further, "Say something more." At that instant, Basho heard the plop of a frog jumping into a pond, so he answered, "Frog jumps in / The sound of water." In Japanese, the poem consists of seven and five syllables; being a poet, Basho naturally expressed it as a poem. And Buccho Zenji approved his realization. Later Basho told his senior students, "I want you to add a phrase of five syllables to the beginning of this." Somehow Basho didn't like any of the lines they came up with and added this first line himself: "Old pond."

Zen Master Sengai (1750–1837), whose paintings have become famous in this country through the work of D. T. Suzuki, painted a picture of a frog and accompanied it with the following poem:

Old pond,
Basho jumps in—
The sound of water.

Another time he drew a picture of a frog and wrote:

Old pond,
Frog jumps in–
The sound.

"Of water" was eliminated. Another poet by the name of Shiken Taguchi saw Sengai's painting and complained, "This is not a haiku." Sengai replied, "Yes, I know. I want you to hear the sound."

Isn't that a nice story? What kind of sound is it?

In the first poem, Sengai says that Basho jumps in. It's easy to see that Sengai sees no division between Basho, himself, and the splash made by the frog. In other words, the subject-object relationship has disappeared. Then Sengai says further, "Frog jumps in / The sound." Here, Sengai is not expressing just one particular sound, but he is manifesting himself as the sound of everything, the form of everything, the color of everything.

Buddhism is the teaching of awakening, the way of enlightenment. And enlightenment is the realization of the unity and harmony of ourselves and externals. It is the way of awakening from a bad dream in which we separate ourselves from everything and everybody, creating all kinds of problems and difficulties. In short, enlightenment is realizing this sound, the sound of oneself, the sound of one's true nature.

What did Shakyamuni realize twenty-five-hundred years ago, when he saw the morning star after six years of meditation on the true nature of life? In the first chapter of the *Denkoroku (The Record of Transmitting of the Light)*, Keizan Zenji writes: "Shakyamuni Buddha, seeing the morning star and attaining the Way, exclaimed, 'I and the great earth and all beings have simultaneously accomplished the Way.'" What does this mean? We can say that Basho saw this morning star when he heard the sound of the water. Our practice is to hear this sound, to see this form. We can express it as this "soundless sound," this "formless form."

This formless form is not something that we can't see, but rather the opposite. Our very form and the form of everything in the universe is nothing but this formless form.

In the Avatamsaka Sutra, it is said that one is all, all is one. And in the Lotus Sutra *(Saddharma Pundarika Sutra)*, it says, "All Dharmas are reality itself." To see this is the moment of enlightenment.

Regarding the Lotus Sutra, I still recall quite vividly that when I was studying under Watanabe Genshu Zenji, the Chief Abbot of Sojiji, he told me that the very spirit, the very essence expressed in the Lotus Sutra is "To penetrate deep into samadhi and see the buddhas in the ten directions." And Dogen Zenji says, "To clarify life and death is of vital importance." In the Lotus Sutra, this grave importance is explained as "opening the eye of Buddha's wisdom." Zen Master Shitou Xiqian (J. Sekito Kisen), Dharma grandson of the Sixth Ancestor, also clearly states, "The important matter is to awaken Buddha's wisdom."

Sometimes we hear it said that we shouldn't seek after enlightenment. What this really means is that we shouldn't seek enlightenment outside ourselves. But we've got to seek *ourselves*, who we really are. That's what all the Ancestors and masters did. Without seeking and searching, we won't get anywhere. So please, take the time to patiently and diligently clarify this grave matter.

As to the characteristics of Soto and Rinzai practice, we can say that the Rinzai school tends to emphasize the importance of attaining and clarifying enlightenment, while in the Soto school, we emphasize the importance of practice itself. This doesn't mean that we don't need to realize the Buddha's wisdom; it's a starting point, but there is still further to go. That's what Dogen Zenji means in the *"Fukanzazengi" (Universal Promotion of the Principles of Zazen)* when he says: "Though you are proud of your understanding and replete with insight, getting hold of the wisdom that knows at a glance, though you attain the way and clarify the mind, giving rise to the spirit that assaults the heavens, you may loiter in the precincts of the entrance and still lack something of the vital path of liberation." Dogen Zenji is not putting down enlightenment; he is just saying that it is not a final accomplishment. In his time, the general tendency was that having attained enlightenment, people didn't practice any longer, and even believed that they could do whatever they wanted. His statement warns against such a tendency. There is no end to how much we can accomplish.

Let us appreciate the following analogy of the poor man and the millionaire from the Lotus Sutra. It is a wonderful metaphor for our practice and how enlightenment can be achieved and deepened.

The son of a millionaire leaves his father's home and starts wandering. The father's house, with its limitless wealth, is the house of the Buddha, our own house. In other words, we have left the home of our true self.

Soon the son becomes poor and experiences all sorts of pain and suffering, while his father spends year after year worrying and searching for him. Finally, after many years spent wandering around, the son happens to appear in front of the very house where he was raised, but it's been so long he can't even recognize it. In fact, such a huge, gorgeous house intimidates him, yet he is curious and starts looking around.

His father happens to see him, and even though the son has changed quite a bit, the father immediately recognizes him and sends his servants to bring him in. But seeing people coming out from the gate and approaching him, the son thinks they've come to catch him because he's been hanging around, and he starts to run away. The messengers go back and report this to the father, and ask, "Should we grab him and bring him in or not?" The father says, "No, don't go after him. We'll have someone dressed the way he is go after him and tell him, 'The boss of that house is a very kind man. We are working there, and he wants you to come and work with us. You don't need to worry about where to stay and what to eat.'" The son agrees, and though still hesitant, enters the house.

Relating again to practice, many people begin and drop out. Those who are unsure about practice could be compared to the son entering the house, so entering the zendo and sitting parallels the son starting to work in the home.

The father gradually promotes his son. In the same way, year after year, in our practice, we use all kinds of expedient means, such as koans, and we mature, little by little. By doing zazen, we become stronger.

After years of work, the son settles in quite nicely, just as after years of practice, we, too, begin to settle. The father asks his son to take care of all financial matters, putting him in charge of practically everything. But still the son doesn't consider that all these treasures are his own; they still seem like someone else's. Finally, when the time ripens and the son is ready, the father reveals the truth. By this time it is not a surprise for the son at all. This moment can be compared to the moment of enlightenment. Prior to this time, the son must have been aware of progressing to higher positions, of becoming more and more confident and capable of dealing with people and handling things.

However, succeeding to the position of overseer is not quite sufficient; attaining enlightenment is not quite sufficient. What remains? Again, our path is wonderfully paralleled in this story. For example, one who acts bossy is not really a master. Growing into that position, digesting all sorts of experiences, one becomes more and more subdued, more understanding, more sympathetic. Finally, one becomes fully mature as the master. The same is true of our practice. After attaining enlightenment or after succeeding to the Dharma, we are still green. We have to grow further and further, until all our rough qualities are polished and our glaring qualities are subdued. Thus we become one with the whole family, the whole society. Then we are really the masters, and our practice, our life, is truly accomplished.

Now let's look at a poem by Dogen Zenji titled "The Lotus Sutra":

> When you grasp
> The heart of this sutra,
> Even the voices
> Of selling and buying in the marketplace
> Expound the Dharma.

When you grasp the heart of this sutra . . . "Heart" could also be translated as "mind." . . . even the voices of selling and buying in the marketplace expound the Dharma. Dogen Zenji is referring as well to the sounds of cars passing in the street, birds chirping in the backyard, dogs barking, kids yelling, helicopters buffeting the wind overhead, all are nothing but "expounding the Dharma."

How do we realize the mind of this sutra? In the Diamond Sutra (Vajracchedika Sutra), there is the expression, "All buddhas and

buddhas' teachings arise from this sutra." What is "this sutra"? It is
buddha nature, true self. The Diamond Sutra also states: "If one tries to
see the Tathagata through forms and voices, he cannot see the Tathagata." Again, what does that mean? If we try to see it, we can't see it: in
a way, this is our dilemma. When we try to see an "it," the seer and the
seen are separate, there is a subject/object relationship; that's how the
usual level of consciousness works. It's not that dichotomy or dualism
itself is wrong. In a way everything is dualistic: enlightenment and delusion, heaven and earth, man and woman, husband and wife, parents and
children, teacher and student, right and left, right and wrong, night and
day, ignorance and wisdom. The point is that we should *transcend*
dichotomy and see the underlying unity of all things.

Bankei Zenji was a Japanese Rinzai master who lived about 250 years
ago and was a friend of Tenkei Denson Zenji, an Ancestor in the Soto
lineage. One day Bankei Zenji said to a group of people, "You are here
to listen to my talk and I am talking to you. You should understand what
I tell you. What is this mind? A dog is barking outside. When you hear
that dog, you are not trying to do anything; you just perceive it. That is
the mind of the Buddha." This is so true: without trying to do anything,
we are living quite satisfactorily. We see something; we naturally
respond. We hear something; we naturally respond. We do something;
we naturally just do it. Then there is no problem. In other words, let consciousness work as consciousness. But somehow we always add something extra to it, and this generates problems. In a sense, our practice is
to trim these extras.

Zen Master Wumen Huikai (J. Mumon Ekai) advises those working
on the koan Mu to trim all thinking and self-consciousness and just put
themselves entirely into "Mu." Dogen Zenji says the same thing: "Cut
off consciousness at its root." In other words, become plainly, genuinely
yourself. Such a state is often compared to a mirror. Explaining the passage in the Heart Sutra, "Not stained, not pure," Master Bankei says
that a mirror just reflects a dog's droppings, and when we remove those
droppings, no stain is left on the mirror. It reflects a beautiful flower, and
when we remove it, no purity is left. He says the same thing of "no
increase, no decrease." A heavy thing is reflected in the mirror, but no
heavy thing remains. No light thing, no big thing, no small thing

remains. That's what's called "no mind" or "no self." When we are truly open and unconditioned by any ideas or standards, we live right here.

I am reminded of the famous passage by Dogen Zenji: "To study the self is to forget the self," which means to become a clear mirror. In this way, we can reflect everything as it is, we can be "enlightened by all things." No division exists, just unity and harmony. Such harmony or unity isn't static; it's active. Sometimes the practice of Zen is like climbing a mountain. Without the climbing, we can't really understand how splendid it is to stand on the mountain peak. Also, we can't know how wonderful and difficult it is to climb to the top. The top of the mountain could be compared to the accomplishment of enlightenment; staying there is static and useless, a big trap, so we have to come down. In the Surangama Sutra, fifty traps are listed, and the worst of them is to think that you have accomplished enough.

We have to descend from the mountain to share our delight with other people and encourage them to climb it themselves. First, we start from home, which is ourself. Dogen Zenji says, "To study Buddhism is to study the self." That's our starting point. "To study the self is to forget the self." That's climbing. "To forget the self is to be enlightened by all things." That's reaching the summit. After attaining enlightenment, we must embody wisdom as compassion. This is the hard part. This is what Dogen Zenji means when he says: "This traceless enlightenment continues endlessly." In other words, seeing everything and everybody as part of ourselves, we take good care of them. I would especially like to emphasize the importance of taking care; each of us should really make this her or his practice. Regardless of how much or how little we accomplish, whatever we do, we use both wisdom and compassion. This is what I want you to be really aware of.

Why is it necessary to help or to save other people? It is important to understand how life goes. From the intrinsic standpoint, all of us are buddhas, but somehow we aren't really satisfied that this is true. We have to actually experience it, really see for ourselves how true it is. But even seeing it is not enough; we have to practice continuously. That's what Dogen Zenji calls the circle of continuous practice: raising the bodhi mind, practicing, achieving enlightenment, and attaining nirvana. Practice goes on in this way forever.

Amitabha Buddha said, "Until everybody is enlightened, I won't enter into perfect nirvana." In the Vimalakirti Sutra, the layman Vimalakirti says, "I am sick because people are sick." And in the Rinzai school, we use the koan, Master Boyan's (J. Hakuun's) "not yet, not enough." However much we accomplish, still it's insufficient, incomplete. So what is enlightenment?

Soen Nakagawa Roshi composed a haiku at the beginning of the year of the Dragon (1976) which I thought might be a nice way to end this chapter on enlightenment:

Ascend the slope,
Descend that very slope—
Spring of the dragon.

2: Sudden and Gradual Enlightenment

Taizan Maezumi

L IFE ALWAYS PRESENTS US with pairs. There are always two aspects that complement each other: sun and moon, day and night, mother and father, life and death. How easily our mind becomes occupied in a one-sided way! When we see one aspect and ignore the other, somehow we feel incomplete and the circumstances of our lives seem insufficient.

We can talk about aspects of our Zen practice as appearing in pairs, like enlightenment and delusion, or the relative and absolute points of view, or sudden and gradual teachings. We tend to set one side against the other and compare them. When we look closely, we can see that each pair is always just two aspects of one thing. Seeing this one thing, we can appreciate each aspect in a better way.

Dogen Zenji said of the five schools of Zen in China, "Although the five schools are different, they all transmit one Buddha Mind." He said that we shouldn't even look upon Zen as a sect. The point is that we should genuinely understand and realize this One Buddha Mind. Dogen Zenji says all kinds of beautiful things about it, but we should really penetrate this One Buddha Mind ourselves.

When Dogen Zenji returned from China, he said, "I have returned empty-handed, without the smallest bit of Buddhadharma." "Empty-handed"—when you've got nothing in your hands, they are free to be used in the best way. And "without the smallest bit of Buddhadharma" — in other words, everything *is* the Buddhadharma. It's not a matter of having it or not: this very life, as it is, is nothing but the Buddhadharma itself.

In Buddhism, there has been much discussion of the issue of sudden and gradual approaches to practice. In fact, after the Sixth Ancestor, this became a very controversial topic of debate among people practicing Zen. But the issue of sudden and gradual is not a matter of one or the other; in some way or another, our practice includes both sudden and gradual aspects. If we don't get attached to just one side, we can appreciate the sudden and gradual aspects from a number of different perspectives. Usually the sudden aspect of practice is understood to be the moment of the enlightenment experience, *kensho* or *satori*, which always happens suddenly. This sudden enlightenment experience is of crucial importance, but we should also appreciate the gradual practice that leads up to that moment, and the gradual practice of deepening, refining, and clarifying our vision after the enlightenment experience. *Kensho* means "to see the nature," the buddha nature. To experience kensho is to see that this life, as it is, is the very life of the Buddha. Even though our life is the enlightened way itself, because our understanding is not quite right, we somehow don't see that this is so. The Rinzai school especially emphasized the importance of having this sudden opening.

In his commentary on the koan Mu, Master Wumen (J. Mumon) says:

> Concentrate yourself into *Mu*, making your whole body, with its 360 bones and 84,000 pores, one great question. Day and night, without ceasing, keep digging into it. Do not interpret it as "nothingness" or as "being" or "nonbeing." It must be like a red-hot iron ball which you have gulped down and which you try to vomit up, but cannot. Cast away all delusive thoughts and feelings which you have cherished up to the present. After a while, your efforts will come to fruition naturally, and inside and out will become one. You will then be like a dumb person who has had a wonderful dream: he knows it within himself but he cannot speak of it. Suddenly *Mu* breaks open and astonishes the heavens and shakes the earth.... Though you may stand on the brink of life and death, you will enjoy the great freedom. In the six realms and the four modes of birth, you will live in the *samadhi* of innocent play.

It's not a matter of intellectually figuring out what *Mu* is. To see *Mu* you must put yourself completely into it until you are *Mu* itself. Concentrate on *Mu* until you and *Mu* become one thing, and then keep on working. Then, as Wumen says, "suddenly *Mu* breaks open" and you will realize that from the beginning you are nothing but *Mu*, the buddha nature itself.

We call this experience *shokan*, the first barrier. Passing this first barrier is to experience the same realization that all the buddhas and masters experienced themselves. But there are many degrees of realization—sometimes it is deep, sometimes shallow, sometimes the vision is clear, sometimes cloudy. In fact, usually this first opening is just a glimpse of the enlightened state. Having passed this first barrier, practice continues as you deepen, enlarge, and polish this wisdom. We study 600 or 700 koans; but you could also just continue with one koan. The point is not the number of koans, the point is to see clearly what this life really is. The Buddha Way is boundless, and its accomplishment and actualization goes on endlessly.

In the Soto School we also appreciate gradual practice and sudden realization. But Soto Zen emphasizes that because this life is altogether one—the Buddha Way itself—you should not expect kensho. As soon as you chase after kensho, right there you create a subject-object dichotomy. Many people misunderstand, saying that the Soto school is not concerned with the enlightenment experience. This is nonsense. Awakening is the very core of the Buddha's teaching, but if we are *thinking about* awakening, we are separating ourselves from it.

So how do we practice without being dualistic? This is what Dogen Zenji expresses in the famous passage from the *"Genjokoan"*:

> To study Buddhism is to study the self.
> To study the self is to forget the self.
> To forget the self is to be enlightened by the
> ten thousand dharmas.

When you really are just yourself, you forget the self. And when the self is forgotten, the Buddhadharma instantaneously reveals itself as the whole of life—the life of each of us. So in studying the self, in practicing zazen, put yourself completely into just being zazen. In following the breath, just be the breath; in working on a koan, be the koan; if you do shikantaza, completely be shikantaza.

Practicing in this way, the subject-object dichotomy will fall away and you will have a glimpse of your true nature. But this is not all. Dogen Zenji goes on to say:

> *To be enlightened by the ten thousand dharmas*
> *Is to free one's body and mind and those of others.*
> *No trace of enlightenment remains,*
> *And this traceless enlightenment is continued forever.*

Having seen your own true nature, that awareness then expands to include everything, and the Buddhadharma functions without hindrance as oneself and others. Going still further, beyond any trace of enlightenment and non-enlightenment, being completely ordinary, traceless enlightenment continues accomplishing itself endlessly.

So we can see sudden and gradual aspects in both Soto and Rinzai practice. We can say it is a continuous process: first practice, then sudden realization, then further practice and further realization continuing endlessly. From a lifelong perspective, the gradual and sudden aspects together could be seen as a gradual process.

In Soto Zen we also emphasize the intrinsic point of view. In other words, from the beginning, practice and realization are one. Practice is this life, and realization is this life, and this life is revealed right here and now *as* each of us. Realization is nothing other than seeing this plain fact. Whether we realize it or not, it is the reality. Whether we practice five years or ten years or not at all, it is the plain fact. In each moment the Buddhadharma is completely revealed as this life. Every instant appears and disappears as the absolute truth. What could be more sudden than this?

Whether we know it or not, this life is an abundant treasure house. The trouble is that, instead of taking care of it in the best way, we are practically strangling ourselves with it. This is why Dogen Zenji says, "This Dharma is amply present in every person, but unless one practices it is not manifested, unless there is realization it is not attained. It is not a question of one or many; let loose of it and it fills your hands. It is not bounded vertically or horizontally; speak it and it fills your mouth."

There is a beautiful expression in Spanish, *poco a poco,* little by little. Our life is always *poco a poco,* and the way we practice *poco a poco* is zazen. In each moment, in each little-by-little step, the Buddha-dharma is completely revealed. So little is not little, it is boundless.

Instead of just talking about this or that and getting caught in extremes, how do we take care of the two sides? I'll leave it to you. Our practice is always *poco a poco.* If you say it is little by little, fine. If you say gradual, fine. If you say sudden, that's fine, too.

II: Delusion

3: "Yunmen's Two Sicknesses"

CASE 11 OF THE *BOOK OF EQUANIMITY*

Translated by Taizan Maezumi and Dana Fraser

EDITORS' NOTE: The *Book of Equanimity* (also published as the *Book of Serenity;* Ch. *Cong-Rong lu;* J. *Shoyoroku*) is a koan collection of 100 cases compiled in Song Dynasty China by the Soto Zen master Tiantong Hongzhi (J. Wanshi Shogaku, 1091–1157). Following the example of Master Xuedou Chongxian (J. Setcho Juken) (980–1052), compiler of the *Blue Cliff Record*, Master Hongzhi wrote an appreciatory verse for each case. Several generations later, Master Wansong Xingxiu (J. Bansho Gyoshu) added a preface and a long commentary to each koan and composed capping phrases (*jakugo;* shown here in parentheses) for the main case and appreciatory verse. We have included all but the long commentary to "Yunmen's Two Sicknesses" here.

Preface to the Assembly

The bodiless person is ill. The handless person makes medicine. The mouthless person eats meals. The senseless person is well. Tell me, for incurable disease, what's the treatment?

Main Case

Attention! Great Master Yunmen said, "When the light doesn't penetrate completely, there are two kinds of sickness. (Master Wansong: *Do you feel your mouth dry up and tongue shrivel?*) One sickness is when you are not quite clear and there is something in front of you. (Master

Wansong: *When you see a ghost in the daylight, isn't it an illusion?*)
Even though you thoroughly penetrate the emptiness of all dharmas,
there still seems to be something. In this also, the light has not penetrated completely. *(Already your chest is constricted. What does it matter if your throat is closed?)*

"There are also two kinds of sickness in the Dharmakaya. (Master
Wansong: *Calamities don't happen alone.*) The first is when you reach
the Dharmakaya. If dharma-attachment is not forgotten and a view of
self still persists, you plummet into the Dharmakaya side. (Master Wansong: *Not only are there false idols outside, there's also one within.*)
Though you penetrate this, if you are negligent, it's still not good. (Master Wansong: *Nursing sickness, you lose your body.*) Even after minute
examination, if you say, 'What inadequacy could there be!'—this is the
second sickness." *(Before the doctor's gone out the door, already you're
having another seizure.)*

Appreciatory Verse

> *Multitudes of shapes allowed to be as is.*
> (Master Wansong: Let them be! How could they annoy you!
> If you understand them, they won't harm you.)
> *Boundless, thorough liberation still obstructs the eye.*
> (Master Wansong: The wandering eye follows the sparkler.)
> *To sweep out this garden, who has the strength?*
> (Master Wansong: Erasing traces leaves marks, the more you
> rub the more it shows.)
> *Concealed in one's heart, it gives rise to feelings.*
> (Master Wansong: Doubt in the mind creates ghosts in the dark.)
> *Autumn mist, a boat on the water.*
> (Master Wansong: Submerged in stagnant water.)
> *A boat with light pole motionless among the reeds.*
> (Master Wansong: The still shore deceives people.)
> *An old fisherman with skewered perch thinks of going to market.*
> (Master Wansong: Selling his catch, he makes a profit.)
> *Carefree, a leaf sails over the waves.*
> (Master Wansong: Finding the subtlety, following the stream.)

4: Sitting Down in the World of Enlightenment

COMMENTARY ON "YUNMEN'S TWO SICKNESSES"

Hakuun Yasutani

YUNMEN (J. UMMON) is Zen Master Wenyan (J. Bun'en), who lived on Mt. Yunmen in Guanzhou province. He visited Venerable Muzhou (J. Bokushu) and had an initial clarification of the great matter of life and death. Afterwards, under Zen Master Xuefeng Yicun (J. Seppo Gison), he exhausted the essential mystery and became a Dharma heir of Xuefeng.

Eight koans of Yunmen appear in the *Book of Equanimity* and eighteen in the *Blue Cliff Record*. Yunmen undoubtedly holds a most important position with respect to Zen teaching. He is the founder of the Yunmen school, an important lineage though now no longer extant.

Since Yunmen describes four types of Zen sickness in the Main Case, old man Wansong (J. Bansho) focuses on that and in his Preface to the Assembly sets forth four kinds of sickness.

The bodiless person is ill. The handless person makes medicine. The mouthless person eats. The senseless person is well. What is this? What it says is nothing at all extraordinary. A bodiless person is one who, having dropped off mind and body, has opened his eyes. He is a person who is no longer afflicted in body and mind. The view of "things" and "self" has been totally removed. It's peace of mind and quietness of spirit. This is no doubt an important matter, but become attached to it and it becomes an illness. This is "a bodiless person suffering illness."

The handless person makes medicine. Being handless, one can finally hold things and release them. When the hands are being used naturally, things can freely be held and put down. A person who is handless has dropped off mind and body. In addition to the whole world being "the bright light of your Self and the color of dropped-off mind and body," heaven is heaven, earth is earth, what is, is—it's a world where there is no lack. Compared to the bodiless person, being handless is more splendid, but become attached to it and, as you might expect, it becomes an illness.

The mouthless person eats. It's the same as with the handless person, but has greater degrees of depth and shallowness. It is a more acute sickness. Take note that it is written "eats," not "takes medicine." The one who "takes meals" has a sickness so subtle that he doesn't even know he needs medicine.

What sort of person is a senseless or a nonreceiving person? In Buddhism, to receive is to suffer. Whether glory or status, authority or wealth, to receive any of them is an occasion for suffering. People often think receiving is a pleasure; but it's a "topsy-turvy pleasure." And yet, to run away, wishing not to receive anything at all, is merely what a small-minded practitioner does. The Mahayana bodhisattva receives, but receives without attachment. Being unattached, one can, for the first time, appropriately and freely receive. That is real peace and comfort.

Receive everything; be unattached to everything. Unattached, you can manage everything. This is the nonreceiving person. Although not yet great liberation, it's the place of truly great peace and comfort. However, this at once becomes the great-peace-and-comfort sickness. Become stuck even to a comfortable chair, and it becomes a painful affliction.

Tell me, for incurable disease, what's the treatment? With the question of treating these four difficult diseases, Wansong comes to the Main Case.

> *Attention! Great Master Yunmen said, "When the light doesn't penetrate completely, there are two kinds of sickness. One sickness is when you are not clear and there is something in front of you."*

Great Teacher Yunmen describes the four types of harmful influences in Zen training by first separating them into two general kinds and then further into two specific forms of each.

"Light" is enlightenment, the bright light of your own Self. Although you may be enlightened, if it is not great enlightenment, it will be hazy. This is called "light doesn't penetrate completely." In this category, there are two kinds of sickness. In one of them, the light isn't penetrating everywhere, and so you think that there are objects in front of you.

Before becoming enlightened, you just think that you are here and things that are not you are over there, and you are unable to take even one step out of a dualistic world. Experience enlightenment, even shallow enlightenment, and you naturally understand that the thought of "objects over there" is completely mistaken. You have opened your eyes to a world in which the totality is yourself. This is enlightenment.

Just to understand that oneself and others are the same is not yet complete enlightenment. As it says in the poem "The Identity of Relative and Absolute" (J. *Sandokai*): "To encounter the absolute is not yet enlightenment." To experience that all ten directions of the world are the whole body of your Self is enlightenment. When enlightenment is thorough, it is definite that there is nothing outside of oneself, but when enlightenment is not thorough, then this fact of enlightenment is not clear at all times and in all places. Somehow, you cannot help thinking that there still seems to be something other than yourself. This is the first sickness.

"Even though you thoroughly penetrate the emptiness of all dharmas, there still seems to be something. In this also, the light has not penetrated completely."

Here another sickness is revealed. With regard to this, first keep in mind what is called "person emptied" and "dharmas emptied." "Person emptied" is only tentatively achieved. Therefore things that are not oneself seem to be outside of you. That is because the state of "dharmas emptied" has not been achieved.

When both person and dharmas are emptied, there doesn't seem to be anything remaining at all, but deeply hidden, something still not empty somehow remains like a thin haze. As if a bit of cloud remains, the vast sky is not yet clear. That's proof that, in truth, the bottom of the bucket is not yet broken through. If a cloud even the size of a hair remains, it expands anew, becoming a whole body of cloud. So do not be inattentive. If you are inattentive here, your dwelling in this realm immediately becomes a sickness.

> *"There are also two kinds of sickness in the Dharmakaya. The first is when you reach the Dharmakaya. If dharma-attachment is not forgotten and a view of self still persists, you plummet into the Dharmakaya side."*

The two previous kinds of sickness derive from the light's not having penetrated thoroughly. In the two now to be revealed, the light truly does penetrate thoroughly. This is the stage at which "Above the earth and below heaven, I alone am the revered one." The Dharmakaya is the real Self; to arrive at the Dharmakaya is to be awakened to the real Self. This is thoroughgoing great enlightenment.

In reality, though great enlightenment is thoroughly penetrated, joy remains. Following on that is the sickness of "So many people don't know of this world that I so appreciate and revere." This sickness is called "Attachment to the dharma of enlightenment." The view of self discussed here is different from the ordinary view of ego. Having a mental picture of enlightenment from the perspective of your own wisdom is called "a view of self persisting." Therefore there is a plummeting into the Dharmakaya side, and a sitting down in the world of enlightenment. This is enlightenment-sickness.

> *"Though you penetrate this, if you are negligent, it's still not good. Even after minute examination, if you say, 'What inadequacy could there be!'—this is the second sickness."*

Being able to penetrate through is thoroughgoing great enlightenment. It is entry into the Dharmakaya realm, and to discard this too is to be cured. For example, having had thoroughgoing great enlightenment and having discarded it and thereby been cured, occasionally you fall again into the Dharmakaya side, or a view of self arises and stays for a while without being discarded. If with all your might from moment to moment you go on paying close attention, you can't go wrong. This is, "However you look at it there's no inadequacy." But sit down here and this too will be a sickness. With that, all four kinds of "sitting down" have been set forth. Whenever there is sitting down there is sickness, there is failure. If you don't sit down anywhere, whether your practice be profound or shallow, whether your enlightenment be bright or dim, however you happen to be, you will naturally accord with the Way.

How about it? Sickness that you never thought could be so subtle has in this fashion been clearly, definitely diagnosed and plucked out. Unless you have quite a doctor, you won't get treatment this complete. Great Teacher Yunmen, as you might expect, is the king of all the great doctors in the Zen world. If those people who have "one-piece enlightenment" and come to realization after realization do not fully and freely perspire over sober-minded and honest koans such as this, their realization will not be authentic. It is most remarkable that the *Book of Equanimity* has delicate koans like this.

Let's examine the appreciatory verse:

> *Multitudes of shapes allowed to be as is.*
> *Boundless, thorough liberation still obstructs the eye.*
> *To sweep out this garden, who has the strength?*
> *Concealed in one's heart, it gives rise to feelings.*
> *Autumn mist, a boat on the water.*
> *A boat with light pole motionless among the reeds.*
> *An old fisherman with skewered perch thinks of going*
> *   to market.*
> *Carefree, a leaf sails over the waves.*

Multitudes of shapes allowed to be as is. What are these multitudes of shapes? Don't just look over there, thinking it's the ten thousand things of heaven and earth. What is called "multitudes of shapes" is the sum total of all manifest shapes, as well as the realms of subjective and objective insight. The Chinese characters translated "as is" mean "to have the appearance of a high mountain." What is "allowed to be"? It is to have no shortcomings. Mountains are high, rivers are long. A long thing is long Dharmakaya, a short thing is short Dharmakaya. Female is complete and male is complete. In differences, are there any insuffi- ciencies? Or rather than insufficiencies, doesn't difference constitute their absolute value? If differences vanish, existing value also vanishes. Let's mix sweet rice cake and flavored rice in a hodgepodge and see. Wouldn't the value of both the rice cakes and the flavored rice be negated? I was impressed to hear of a Pure Land practitioner who, having experienced the compassion of Amitabha Buddha, responded, "Oh, thank you," when told that "the length of the crane's leg is as it is" and "the shortness of the duck's leg is as it is" are salvation itself. To see this world of no shortcom- ings is a leaping, first-rate awakening. But this awakening itself can at once become a sickness, as the following line indicates.

Boundless, thorough liberation still obstructs the eye. "Boundless, thorough liberation" is the exact opposite of "multitudes of shapes." To be thoroughly liberated is for there to be neither the three times nor the ten directions. It's "originally there's not one thing." No delusion, no enlightenment, no everything, no nothing. No fringe of cloud obstruct- ing the eye. Compared with "multitudes of shapes," it is an enlighten- ment one stage more profound. However, this enlightenment at once becomes a sickness and obstructs the eye.

To sweep out this garden, who has the strength? To sweep the gar- den is to sweep out all the rubbish in one's head, to sweep out the sick- ness of enlightenment. This should be examined together with the following line.

Concealed in one's heart, it gives rise to feelings. Here *one* does not refer to someone else. "One" is each person, each individual. "In one's heart" is within the breast. "Gives rise to feelings" means to think: "That principle is thus-and-so"; "this principle is thus-and-so." Such thinking is done even if you do not intend to, and so it is "concealed." This dharma-attachment is exceedingly difficult to remove. Such feel- ings just arise. This is the sickness called "incurable disease."

Autumn mist, a boat on the water.
A boat with light pole motionless among the reeds.

Here at long last, the poet begins to sing of a pure, refreshing state, a state of no impediments, no attachments, nothing to interfere, nothing insufficient. This is exemplified by the autumn scenery. In autumnal countryside on a quiet river rests a boat. Both sky and water are blue. On the bank, reed-flowers glisten white as snow. The boat has been laid with its bow on the shore and just left there. It's an utterly peaceful world where nothing needs to be done. This is called "extinction manifests." It's the realm of "great peace on earth." It is the real state of nirvana. But this too is a sickness. Stop here even a little and you will be "a dead person at the ultimate."

> *An old fisherman with skewered perch thinks of going*
> *to market.*
> *Carefree, a leaf sails over the waves.*

Previously, you boarded the boat in order to save yourself, but now you *are* the boat sailing to save others. *"Skewered perch"* are sea bream speared on a skewer. *"An old fisherman"* is a fish-catching grandfather in whom all inclinations have been eliminated. He searches for customers with the fish he's taken, crying, "Come buy, come buy. I'm waiting for a bid. I'll sell for a fair price." Carefree, isn't he! He isn't an insistent salesman. He does not discount. To do either would destroy the Buddhadharma. *"A leaf"* means a small boat. A boat bobs on the long river, going *"squeak-thud, squeak-thud"* as it rows along. Always, in this place or that, just right, just right, becoming one with it, carrying across donkeys, carrying across horses—that's the aspect of teaching freely. The initial line of the verse is Manjusri's wisdom; the concluding line is Avalokitesvara's compassion. United, wisdom and compassion are complete.

5: "Ghosts in the Daylight"
COMMENTARY ON THE CAPPING PHRASES
Taizan Maezumi

YUNMEN MENTIONS two kinds of sickness, but if we carefully examine the case we see a number of different stages which come after attaining some understanding. The first of these sicknesses is called "the sickness of not attaining." You run around in your head, dissatisfied and uncertain, attempting to do or see something. You may wonder, "What is Zen? It sounds interesting," and then you might try it. Still the mind is wandering here and there. Then you come to a certain realization, and yet not being quite sure of your understanding, you tend to be attached to it. These are two kinds of initial Zen sickness.

This case starts with more advanced sickness. For example, you have a further realization and you free yourself from attachment to it, whereupon you fall into another trap, which is "the sickness of making yourself free." You see, there are all kinds of sickness. We are all originally buddhas, and we don't need to attempt to attain enlightenment as such. We should just sit; everything is here. In a way that's true, and yet it's a very one-sided view. We have to see both sides. One is the absolute side as expressed in the appreciatory verse: *"Multitudes of shapes allowed to be as is."* All phenomena—mountains, rivers, trees, and grasses—are as they are. Some are high, some are low; some small, some big. They are as they are, absolute. Yet being absolute, of the same nature, there are nonetheless differences.

How you practice is very important: how you clearly see sameness and differences; how clearly you see yourself as the sameness and difference; how you share practice with others, and how we all together accomplish the Supreme Way. Since it's a boundless process to begin with, we can't stop anywhere. If we stick to any place, it becomes a sickness. Although Yunmen divides this into several major sicknesses, wherever there are twenty or thirty people, there are twenty or thirty different sicknesses. We need to find a way to proceed from wherever we are. There is a koan which asks, "How do you take a step from the top of a hundred-foot pole?" Wherever you are, whatever you do, taking a step from a hundred-foot pole is the way to proceed.

> *Attention! Great Master Yunmen said, "When the light doesn't penetrate completely, there are two kinds of sicknesses."*

> *Master Wansong's capping phrase: "Do you feel your mouth dry up and your tongue shrivel?"*

I feel like Master Wansong is talking to me. Here he literally refers to Yunmen and, in a way, is saying, "Hey, Master Yunmen, you attained some degree of realization. Don't you feel ashamed of yourself? Mind your own business and leave us alone." But of course by saying this, Wansong directly warns his disciples to realize where they stand and to know what kind of sickness they have.

> *"One sickness is when you are not quite clear and there is something in front of you."*

> *Master Wansong's capping phrase: "When you see a ghost in the daylight, isn't it an illusion?"*

To begin with, altogether the world is one, and being one, what you see is all a part of you. Everything is nothing but you. If you recognize something, it is thus apart from you, like an optical illusion. This is a sickness. Even those who have passed the first barrier do not see this clearly. The Diamond Sutra says that our life is "like dew, like a flash of lightning." You must really see this and contemplate it.

This reminds me of a story about the priest Ryokan, who lived a few hundred years ago in Japan, and whose poems have become quite popular in recent years. Master Ryokan practiced hard when he was young and accomplished quite well under a very famous Soto teacher. Afterward he lived alone in a small hut. Day after day, he did nothing but play with children and talk to people and compose poems. One day he was walking on the roadside in the darkness and felt the need to defecate, so he walked into a potato field by the road and squatted. The owner of the field, who had been watching every night for potato thieves, caught Ryokan and beat him up. Another person who happened to pass by shouted at the field owner, "What are you doing? That's our priest Ryokan. Stop it." Ryokan didn't try to explain anything to the owner; he didn't even apologize. He just let the owner beat him up.

Later, Ryokan's acquaintance asked him, "Why didn't you tell him that you were the priest Ryokan?" Instead of answering, Ryokan wrote this poem:

> *The one who hits and the one who is beaten,*
> *Both are like dew or a flash of lightning.*

In one way or another, the problems that arise for us are due to the dualism of subject and object. In themselves, subject and object are like the right hand and the left hand, man and woman, young and old, high and low, yin and yang, night and day. That's the way it is. The problem is that we become attached to one side or the other; seeing only one side, we lack understanding and can't communicate. We don't see the unity of all opposites, the whole picture. Actually the sicknesses Yunmen lists here are due to our partial, one-sided vision. So in this first sickness—"When you are not quite clear and there is something in front of you..."—we are conditioned by objects and they become our sickness.

> *"Even though you thoroughly penetrate the emptiness of all dharmas, there still seems to be something. In this also, the light has not penetrated completely."*

> *Master Wansong's capping phrase: "Already your chest is constricted. What does it matter if your throat is closed?"*

Within yourself, you empty the dharmas, you realize that all externals are empty, are *Mu*, and yet there is something within you which remains, called true self, emptiness, buddha nature. You feel it. You are still attached to yourself and are conditioned by the subject. This is a sickness. To penetrate the emptiness of all dharmas is not easy. Even if you see the emptiness of all things, still the light hasn't penetrated completely. Wansong says, "Your throat is closed." You ate something, but you can't swallow it. These are two kinds of sickness in the Dharmakaya.

> *"When you reach the Dharmakaya, if dharma-attachment is not forgotten and a view of self still persists, you plummet into the Dharmakaya side."*
>
> *Master Wansong's capping phrase: "Not only are there false idols outside, there's also one within."*

People think that attitudes and problems are caused by forces outside themselves, but we are the ones who create them, even after attaining enlightenment. When attaining enlightenment, you free yourself and take initiative. In doing so, you may become arrogant. Hakuin Zenji says that he had a lot of trouble with his arrogance until he encountered Shoju Rojin, who beat him up.

> *"Even though you thoroughly penetrate the emptiness of all dharmas, there still seems to be something…Though you penetrate this, if you are negligent, it's still not good."*
>
> *Master Wansong's capping phrase: "Nursing sickness, you lose your body."*

Such negligence was quite common during the Song Dynasty in China, which was the main reason that Soto practitioners misunderstood koan study and the Rinzai style of practice. They saw people who, after attaining enlightenment and finishing their studies, thought that they didn't need to do zazen any more. This is a sickness indeed. Many different things have to be observed; we can't be negligent. To cure your sickness, you take the medicine of enlightenment. Your sickness is cured to a certain extent, but there are side effects.

> *"Even after minute examination, if you say, 'What inadequacy could there be!'—this is the second sickness."*

> *Master Wansong's capping phrase: "Before the doctor's out the door, already you're having another seizure."*

Do you get the point? You cure yourself, then you're relieved, but right there, something happens. What is the antidote? Our vows. Wherever we stand, in accord with our understanding of life, we practice the Four Vows as followers of the Buddha Way.

Capping phrases are interesting. In koan study, students are asked to provide capping phrases from time to time to demonstrate how clear their understanding is and how well they can express themselves. Words are a most effective tool, and we should know how to use them. If we use them skillfully, they have tremendous effects. For example, Master Dongshan was once making a pilgrimage, and at a certain monastery, he so thoroughly defeated the head monk in Dharma combat that the head monk committed suicide out of shame. Of course, we shouldn't use words in that way, but we should be careful since words have such power. In everyday life, just by using words, we quite often hurt other people and they hurt us. On the other hand, words can be used effectively to encourage people and make them happy. As part of our practice, let us be mindful of what we say, how we say it, and to whom we are speaking.

Master Hongzhi Zengjue (Tiantong) (J. Wanshi Shogaku), who composed all of the appreciatory verses for the cases in the *Book of Equanimity*, refers to these sicknesses in the verse for this case.

> *Multitudes of shapes allowed to be as is.* Let them be! How could they annoy you! If you understand them, they won't harm you.
> *Boundless, thorough liberation still obstructs the eye.* The wandering eye follows the sparkler.
> *To sweep out this garden, who has the strength?* Erasing traces

leaves marks, the more you rub the more it shows.

Concealed in one's heart, it gives rise to feelings. Doubt in the mind creates ghosts in the dark.

Autumn mist, a boat on the water. Submerged in stagnant water.

A boat with light pole motionless among the reeds. The still shore deceives people.

An old fisherman with skewered perch thinks of going to market. Selling his catch, he makes a profit.

Carefree, a leaf sails over the waves. Finding the subtlety, following the stream.

In the first two lines, he refers to sickness in a rather general way: *Multitudes of shapes allowed to be as is.* This includes all of us too; we are all allowed to be as is. Even the word "allowed" is, in a way, unnecessary; in fact, there is no other way for things to be. Everything, everybody, is just as is. If you really understand this, more than half of the practice is accomplished. But just to realize that all things are as they are is not sufficient. If you really understand it, you'll be quite content and happy, but the more clearly you see things as they are, the more you will feel that you've got to do something for other people with your understanding. This koan quite clearly indicates how we should proceed in our practice.

There is another famous saying: "When the mind ceases searching, everything manifests itself right here." In other words, all sentient beings are buddhas. But somehow we can't accept this fact, we can't be satisfied, because we separate ourselves from the very fact that we are as we are, that things are as things are. In order to satisfy ourselves, we must remove this division and heal our alienation.

As I always say, there are fundamentally no divisions, no conflicts, between Mu, koan study, and shikantaza. Interpreting these practices superficially, we can say all sorts of things, but there is not much difference between the Soto school and the Rinzai school. In a way, dividing Zen into schools is nonsense. Realizing your true self is nothing but seeing yourself as you are. We are constantly changing; everything is changing, and as long as we live, we are just as we are.

So we ask, what are we? What is our unchanging essence? What we think we are, unfortunately, is not what we are, or at most only a very small portion of it. A large amount can't be contained in a small container. Our life is like an iceberg; we can consciously perceive only a small portion of it. The larger portion is under water. If we try to understand our life using our limited knowledge, understanding is impossible. What is our life? As Buddha and all the masters tell us, it's altogether one life. Even saying "one" sounds silly. Since everything is nothing but your life, it's quite all right that some things are big and some are small, some are high and some are low, some are dark and some are light. But since we find it difficult to accept things as they are, we have to practice, and the struggle begins.

The second line relates what happens after struggling: *Boundless, thorough liberation still obstructs the eye.* You try hard to realize that everything is nothing but one. Those who are working on Mu, work on Mu and become one with Mu, and eventually, sooner or later, you will realize Mu. The term translated here as "boundless, thorough liberation" literally means, "liberate yourself in no direction." That "no direction" becomes an obstacle. That freedom itself becomes an obstacle. If you are really free, you don't talk about freedom, you don't pursue freedom. If you enjoy freedom as such, then you are not really quite free; you are still bound by "freedom."

Wansong's capping phrase for the first line of this poem is: "Let them be! How could they annoy you! If you understand them, they won't harm you." In the second line, he says, *"The wandering eye follows the sparkler."* When you twirl a flaming stick, it makes a circle. Even without the flame, if you twirl it rapidly, it leaves a circle in the air. It's an optical illusion. The circle is perceived, but it does not exist. Enlightenment, liberation, is like this. As long as you recognize something, you are not quite liberated yet.

The next line of the poem is: *To sweep out this garden, who has the strength?* What is this garden? The garden around your house is easy to sweep, but the garden of your mind is difficult to care for. The harder you try, the more you upset yourself. In another famous koan, Zhaozhou was once asked by Yanyang (Yanyang Shanxin; J. Genyo Zenshin, n.d.), "How about one who has nothing?" Zhaozhou said, "Cast it away." Yanyang replied, "Having nothing, what is there to cast away?"

(Yanyang has attached himself to nothing; a big trace is left.) Zhaozhou said, "'If so, carry it on!' These koans express an advanced stage of practice, yet I think you can follow them.

"Concealed in one's heart, it gives rise to feelings."

Master Wansong's capping phrase: "Doubt in the mind creates ghosts in the dark."

It's a rather good capping phrase. In a way, the state he's commenting on is a nice one. You are quite confident about your accomplishment, and yet you are not quite clear. As it says in the Main Case, something still remains. When your vision is not quite clear, then you start seeing all sorts of things: true self, real self, big mind, cosmic mind, absolute consciousness. They're all ghosts in the darkness.

Autumn mist, a boat on the water. You just sail the boat on the beautiful lake with its autumn leaves; quite nice, isn't it? However, when you are attached to it, it becomes a sickness. A beautiful autumn scene is like realizing the Dharmakaya. It's tremendously fascinating, and you think that nobody else sees it, nobody else realizes it. This is a very bad sickness. Wansong's capping phrase: "Submerged in stagnant water." In a way, it's not at all stagnant, and yet, when you look at it from a distance, it's stagnant water. It's almost like crawling into a garbage can.

The next line, *A boat with light pole stands motionless among the reed flowers.* If one watches the shore, it may look like it's moving. If you stick to anything in your practice, even the most advanced accomplishment in a way becomes false. Therefore, Master Tiantong expresses in the final two lines how we should proceed in our practice: *An old fisherman with skewered perch thinks of going to market. Carefree, a leaf sails over the waves.* It's interesting to appreciate who the old fisherman is and what the perch is. There are all kinds of sickness, all kinds of lives. Even masters like Yunmen and Bodhidharma skewered them all together on one stick and tried to sell them. To whom? To those who really wanted them.

Carefree, a leaf sails over the waves. Carefree: totally free, without restriction, without urging, proceeding in accord with the environment, the circumstances, and the time in which one lives. Just go with it like a small leaf carried by the stream. Wansong's capping phrase for the old fisherman is, "Selling his catch, he makes a profit. " What is he selling? This profit is priceless. This reminds me of the last stage of the ten ox-herding pictures and also of another famous poem in which an idiot sage is hired to fill up a well with snow. In order to do this sort of work, you have to be carefree; you can't expect anything. As each pile of snow is dumped into the deep well, it immediately melts. But it doesn't matter, we just do it.

Carefree, a leaf sails over the waves. Wansong's capping phrase: "Finding the subtlety, following the stream." I leave that line to you. This is a hard koan but a nice one. I hope all of you will accomplish this far, and enjoy life together.

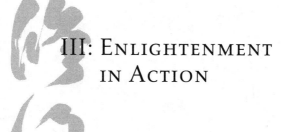

III: Enlightenment in Action

6: "The Eight Awarenesses of the Enlightened Person"

Dogen Zenji's Hachidainingaku

Translated by Taizan Maezumi and Francis Dojun Cook

ALL BUDDHAS are enlightened persons. Enlightened persons have "Eight Awarenesses." To realize these awarenesses is nirvana. Our master, Shakyamuni Buddha, taught the Eight Awarenesses on the night before entering parinirvana.

First: *Having few desires:*
Not seeking too much among the objects of the five desires is
called "having few desires."

The Buddha says: "You monks should know that because those who have many desires search for fame and profit, there is much suffering. Those who have few desires look around less and desire little; therefore they have no such concerns. Practice having few desires. This produces many merits.

"Those who have few desires do not need to ingratiate themselves with others. Also, they withstand the temptations of the senses. One who practices 'having few desires' has neither worry nor fear, but a peaceful mind. Whatever one has is enough, and one never lacks anything. Having few desires is nirvana. This is called 'having few desires.'"

Second: *Knowing how to be satisfied:*
Knowing how much to take is called "knowing how
to be satisfied."

The Buddha says: "You monks should contemplate knowing how to be satisfied if you wish to be liberated from suffering. The Dharma of knowing how to be satisfied is the realm of riches, comfort, peace, and tranquility. Those who know how to be satisfied are happy and comfortable even when sleeping on the ground. Those who do not know how to be satisfied are not satisfied even when dwelling in a heavenly palace. Those who do not know how to be satisfied are poor even though they are wealthy, while those who know how to be satisfied are wealthy even though they have little. Those who do not know how to be satisfied, and are always tempted by the five desires, are consoled by those who know how to be satisfied. This is called 'knowing how to be satisfied.'"

Third: *Enjoying serenity and tranquility:*
Being apart from all disturbances and dwelling alone in a quiet
place is called "enjoying serenity and tranquility."

The Buddha says, "If you seek joy and peace in the serenity and tranquility of non-doing, you should keep away from disturbances and dwell alone in a quiet place. Those who dwell in quiet places are praised and respected by Sakrendra, chief of the gods, and by celestial beings. Therefore, casting away attachment to yourself-and-others, dwell alone in a quiet place and contemplate the cause of suffering. Those who crave the company of other people suffer from their relationship with them, just as a tree will be broken and die when too many birds roost in it. The bondage of worldly involvement will drown you in suffering, just as an old elephant drowns in the mud because he is unable to get out by himself. To liberate oneself from complicated involvements is called non-attachment."

Fourth: *Exerting meticulous effort:*
Exerting oneself meticulously and unceasingly in various
beneficial practices is called "meticulous effort." Be precise,
not careless; go forward, do not regress.

The Buddha says, "If you monks exert meticulous effort, nothing will be difficult to accomplish. Therefore, you should make an effort to practice carefully, for when water flows constantly against a big rock, even a small amount of water will eventually wear a large hole. But if one who practices becomes lax, it will be impossible to accomplish anything. It is like trying to start a fire by rubbing two sticks together; if you stop rubbing before the wood gets hot enough, you can't start a fire. This is what is meant by 'meticulous effort.'"

Fifth: *Not Forgetting Right Thought:*
This is also called "maintaining right thought." "Protecting
the Dharma and not losing it" means "right thought," or "not
forgetting right thought."

The Buddha says: "If you monks seek both a good teacher and good protection and support, nothing is better than 'not forgetting right thought.' For those who do not forget right thought, the thieving multitude of deluding passions cannot break in. For this reason, you should always keep right thought in your mind and regulate it well, for if you lose this thought, all sorts of merits and virtues will be lost. If the power of this thought is strong and firm, then even though you mingle with the thieving five desires, you will not be injured, just as, if you go into battle dressed in armor, you will not fear the enemy. This is the meaning of 'not forgetting right thought.'"

Sixth: *Practicing Samadhi:*
Dwelling in the Dharma undisturbed is what is called "samadhi."

The Buddha says: "When you monks unify your minds, the mind is in samadhi. Since the mind is in samadhi, you know the characteristics of the creation and destruction of the various phenomena in the world. For this reason, you should constantly practice with diligence and cultivate all kinds of samadhi. When you gain samadhi, the mind is not scattered, just as those who protect themselves from floods guard the levee. This is also true for practice. For the sake of the 'water of wisdom,' then, cultivate samadhi well, and do not let it leak. This is called 'samadhi.'"

Seventh: *Cultivating wisdom:*
Wisdom is aroused by hearing, reflecting, practicing, and realizing.

The Buddha says: "When you monks have wisdom, you are without greed. Always reflect upon yourselves; do not lose this wisdom. In this way, you can attain liberation in my Dharma. One who does not is neither a follower of the Way as a monk or layperson, nor is there any other name for such a one. True wisdom is a stout boat which crosses the sea of old age, sickness, and death; it is also a great bright torch in pitch black ignorance; a good medicine for all sick people; a sharp axe which fells the tree of delusion. Therefore, by means of this wisdom which is heard, reflected upon, and practiced, you will increase your merit. When one has the illumination of wisdom, even though one's eyes are merely physical eyes, one is a 'clear-seeing person.' This is what is meant by 'wisdom.'"

Eighth: *Avoiding idle talk:*
Having realization and being free from discrimination is what
is called "avoiding idle talk." To totally know the true form of
all things is the same as being without idle talk.

The Buddha says: "When you monks engage in various kinds of idle talk, your minds are disturbed. Although you have left home and become monks, you are still not liberated. Therefore, you must quickly abandon mind-disturbing idle talk. If you would like to attain the joy of the extinction of delusion, you must first simply extinguish the affliction of idle talk. This is what 'avoiding idle talk' means."

The Buddha says: "You monks should continually and single-mindedly strive to accomplish the Way. Every dharma in the world, whether active or non-active, is characterized by destructibility and unrest. Now please keep quiet and say no more. Time passes on, and I shall enter complete nirvana. This is my final admonition."

These are the Eight Awarenesses of a buddha. Within each one, all eight are contained, thus making a total of sixty-four. Broadly speaking, the number could be infinite, but for the sake of simplicity, sixty-four are enough. This is the final teaching of the Great Master, the revered

Shakyamuni, and it is the ultimate teaching of the Mahayana, spoken at midnight on February fifteenth. He then entered complete nirvana without any further Dharma teaching.

For this reason, disciples of the Tathagata learn and practice these Eight Awarenesses without fail. One who neither knows nor studies nor practices these is not a disciple of the Buddha, for these are the Tathagata's *shobogenzo nehan myoshin* ("treasury of the true Dharma eye, marvelous mind of nirvana"). In spite of this, there are many nowadays who do not know it, and those who have seen it or heard of it are few. Their ignorance of it is due to their being caught up by demons' temptations, and those who did not cultivate enough good roots in previous existences have neither seen it nor even heard of it. In the old days, in the periods of the "true Dharma" and the "imitative Dharma," the Buddha's disciples all knew, studied, and penetrated it. Nowadays, hardly one or two among a thousand monks knows the Eight Awarenesses of the Buddha. How pitiful it is! There is nothing to compare with the barbarians of this decadent time.

However, today the Tathagata's true Dharma is spread over the universe, and the pure Dharma has not yet been extinguished. You must quickly begin to practice it. Don't be sluggish and lazy! It is difficult to encounter the Buddhadharma even after countless eons, and it is also difficult to acquire a human form. Even if you acquire a human body, it is better to be a human being in the three worlds, and even better to have a human form because here one can see the Buddha, hear the Dharma, make one's home-departure, and attain the Way. Those who died before the Tathagata entered final nirvana neither learned nor practiced these Eight Awarenesses of the Buddha. Now we see, hear, learn, and practice them through the power of having cultivated good roots in previous existences. Now, to practice them and increase them in successive lives, to attain peerless enlightenment without fail, and to expound them for the sake of all sentient beings, is to be the same as Shakyamuni Buddha, without any difference.

The "Eight Awarenesses of an Enlightened Person" of the *Shobogenzo* was written at Eiheiji on January 6, 1253. Now, in the year 1255 on the day before the training session ends, Gien has been ordered to make this copy and proofread it. The foregoing essay was written by our late teacher during his last illness. When I reflect upon the fact that the Japanese version of *Shobogenzo* was to be newly rewritten to make one hundred chapters, this becomes the eighty-seventh chapter. After he wrote this, his health gradually declined and he had to give up his writing. Therefore, this text is the very last instruction of our late teacher, and unfortunately, we will not be able to see the intended one hundred chapters. It is most regrettable. Those who love and revere our former teacher should copy and preserve this. This is the final teaching of our late master.

Ejo [Dogen's main disciple] recorded this.

7: Introduction to the Eight Awarenesses

Taizan Maezumi

THESE EIGHT AWARENESSES are a way of looking at the actualization of enlightenment in everyday life. According to the Mahaparinirvana Sutra, the Eight Awarenesses were the final teaching of Shakyamuni Buddha before his death. Interestingly enough, "The Eight Awarenesses of the Enlightened Person" *(Hachidainingaku),* the chapter translated here, was the last chapter of the *Shobogenzo* written by Dogen Zenji before his own death in 1253. By the time this chapter was written, he had attracted a large following of monks to Eiheiji, the monastery built for him in Echizen province by a lay disciple. However, his health had been failing for several years, and we can imagine that he was aware of his impending death and chose these Eight Awarenesses, these very basic aspects of our practice, as the subject of one of his last teishos in order to encourage his disciples.

In many ways, the Eight Awarenesses resemble various other categories and lists that appear in early Indian sutras and are attributed to the Buddha, for example, the eightfold path, the Ten Grave Precepts, and the six paramitas (see glossary). In fact, parallels can be drawn between such lists: the awareness of wisdom can be directly paralleled to "right understanding," which is the first step of the eightfold path; the eighth awareness, "avoiding idle talk," parallels "right speech"; "exerting meticulous effort" corresponds to "right effort"; "samadhi" to "right samadhi"; and so on. Similar parallels might also be drawn with the ten precepts and the six paramitas, but it's not necessary for us to explore them here. Many of these lists were teachings the Buddha presented extemporaneously to his disciples and later recorded and standardized. Consequently, many of the apparent correspondences were actually overlaps or repetitions, because Buddha would often repeat himself by saying very much the same thing in different words.

The Eight Awarenesses are:

1. Having few desires
2. Knowing how to be satisfied
3. Enjoying serenity and tranquility
4. Exerting meticulous effort
5. Not forgetting right thought
6. Practicing samadhi
7. Cultivating wisdom
8. Avoiding idle talk

The Eight Awarenesses also parallel the eightfold path in that we can look at either of them not as a linear progression or as a list of unrelated qualities, but as a spiral which can begin at any point, each stage in turn encouraging the development of the next. For example, if we have few desires, then, of course, we'll find it easier to know how to be satisfied. And knowing how to be satisfied, we will rejoice naturally in the serenity and tranquility that arises in body and mind. Then, having serenity, meticulous effort will arise naturally in the course of our practice. When we exert meticulous effort, we cannot forget right thought. This constant mindfulness and remembrance of who we are—of ourselves as the Three Treasures—encourages the growth of samadhi. And, of course, samadhi turns into wisdom. Interestingly enough, the Eight Awarenesses do not end with wisdom or samadhi, as do similar lists, but with "avoiding idle talk." When we realize that everything is in its very nature empty, then there will be no problem; our talk will not be idle talk. Then having this wisdom and avoiding idle talk, we won't stir up desires unnecessarily and begin the cycle again.

In fact, this cycle closely resembles the spiral of practice described by Dogen Zenji, which begins with raising the bodhi-mind. Raising the bodhi-mind relates to having few desires, knowing how to be satisfied, and enjoying serenity; that is, clearing the path and arousing the aspiration to practice. Then we practice, exerting meticulous effort to remember who we are. Thus, we attain realization, which corresponds to right samadhi, right wisdom, and avoiding idle talk in its deepest sense. After realization, we finally attain nirvana. Then we begin again by throwing away all attainment, raising the bodhi-mind, practicing and realizing. In both the Eight Awarenesses and Dogen Zenji's teaching, the meaning is fundamentally the same: practice endlessly advances; each stage gives rise to and enriches the next. We must beware of getting stuck at any point along the way.

On one level, then, the Eight Awarenesses are a description of how our practice actually proceeds. But even more fundamentally, how should we relate to the Awarenesses? Are they moral or ethical guidelines, or are they actually aspects of the enlightened nature, or a description of the Buddha himself? As the title suggests, these Eight Awarenesses are in fact the awarenesses of the Buddha, or ways of describing the Buddha himself. But again, who is buddha? We ourselves are buddha, and these are ways of appreciating our life and our practice.

One convenient way of looking at the Eight Awarenesses is by using three modes commonly used to interpret the precepts: literal, relational, and intrinsic. According to the literal mode, the precepts are very strictly interpreted; if we do anything that the precepts prohibit, we're violating those precepts. The relational view is much more flexible and appropriate to particular circumstances. Depending on the time, the place, the person or people involved, and the particular circumstances, the precepts are interpreted differently. For example, consider the precept "Do not tell a lie." If you are walking in the woods and a rabbit runs past you, followed by a sport hunter, who asks you, "Which way did the rabbit run?," what will you tell him? At times, what seems like a lie is actually the most appropriate thing to say, according to the time, the place, the person, and the circumstances. The intrinsic view of interpreting the precepts says that there is fundamentally no separation between ourselves and others, and that if we are truly aware of this no-separation and act in accord with it, then it's impossible to violate the precepts. All being intrinsically one, there can be no violation of the precepts.

In the same way, the Eight Awarenesses can be looked at from these three points of view. In one sense, these Eight Awarenesses are strict guidelines for our practice. That is, we must learn how to be satisfied, we must learn to enjoy serenity, we must develop right effort, and we must remember that we are the Three Treasures. From the relational point of view, yes, we should have few desires, but there are times when desires are appropriate. For instance, in practice, we desire to end suffering. Regarding serenity, there are times when we are in the midst of activity and commotion with other people in order to help them in their practice. The same can be said of the other Awarenesses.

As for the intrinsic view, the Awarenesses are indeed the awarenesses of the enlightened person. A buddha, finding no separation between herself and other beings, very naturally acts in this way. Feeling no separation from others, a buddha naturally has few desires. Feeling no separation from others, from our surroundings, from what is happening right now, of course we can't help but be satisfied, enjoying the serenity of life as it is. When we know the oneness of ourselves and others, effort becomes right effort, our activity becomes the embodiment of wisdom, and no talk is idle talk.

With this in mind, let's study each of the Eight Awarenesses, keeping in mind that we're not talking about some distant goal or the life of someone who lived thousands of years ago, but are actually talking about our life right now. Buddha addresses "you monks," but is talking to all of us practitioners, right here, now.

Editor's note: In the chapters that follow, each chapter opens with a translation of text from Dogen Zenji, followed by a commentary on that text by Taizan Maezumi and a discussion with Bernie Glassman.

8: "Having Few Desires"

Dogen Zenji's Text

All buddhas are enlightened persons. Enlightened persons have "Eight Awarenesses." To realize these Awarenesses is nirvana. Our master, Shakyamuni Buddha, taught the Eight Awarenesses on the night before entering parinirvana.

First: *Having few desires:*
Not seeking too much among the objects of the five desires is called "having few desires."

The Buddha says: "You monks should know that because those who have many desires search for fame and profit, there is much suffering. Those who have few desires look around less and desire little; therefore they have no such concerns. Practice having few desires. This produces many merits.

"Those who have few desires do not need to ingratiate themselves with others. Also, they withstand the temptations of the senses. One who practices 'having few desires' has neither worry nor fear, but a peaceful mind. Whatever one has is enough, and one never lacks anything. Having few desires is nirvana. This is called 'having few desires.'"

Maezumi Roshi's Commentary

WHEN WE CAREFULLY examine ourselves, we see all kinds of desires, and yet there is actually nothing to gain. At the same time, there is nothing to lose either. This is the very plain state of existence; our life is always fulfilled in just the right way. We have this life, we live it, and this is enough. In its best sense, having few desires is to realize this. Yet, somehow, we think something is lacking, and so we have all kinds of desires.

Usually when we speak about desire, we mean the five major ones: desire for wealth; material things, which in a narrower sense is a desire for sex, but in a broader sense is a desire for anything which has form; as well as food; fame; and sleep. Of course, there is also the desire to practice, the desire to accomplish the Way. We might call this "right desire," because it arises out of an aspiration to benefit other people before thinking about ourselves.

When we really see the truth of the five desires, we see prajna wisdom. Having prajna wisdom, seeing that there is nothing outside of ourselves, what is there to desire? This is not difficult to appreciate. The less we desire, the fewer problems we have. We often hear people complain that they earn lots of money, and yet all the money disappears. Why? They have more bills to pay, they buy all kinds of gadgets for pleasure. The more they have, the more headaches they have, too. A friend who works at the bank tells me quite often, "These people who have lots of money are so often unhappy. It's painful to watch them." It is so true that if you are satisfied with what you have, you don't need to worry. It's very easy to understand, isn't it?

Another interesting way to understand these desires is to correlate them with our senses: desires of the eye, ear, nose, tongue, body, and consciousness. To say that the senses "want" may seem rather peculiar, but actually our senses create certain desires, being attracted by sounds, smells, sights, tastes, thoughts, and tangible objects. What creates the real difficulty, though, is our ignorance. Why? We are ignorant simply because we don't have right wisdom. What veils right wisdom? Delusions.

There are many delusions, but theoretically, we say there are six basic kinds of delusion: greed, anger, ignorance, conceit, doubt, and wrong views. The first one is greed. The five desires come under this category. Being greedy, we want all kinds of things. The second delusion which clouds wisdom is anger. Having strong likes or dislikes, we can't see clearly. The third delusion is ignorance or folly. In Japanese we say *mumyo,* literally "no light," or "darkness." Since it's dark, you don't know where you are or what you have to do.

The fourth delusion is conceit. The most common conceit is when you think you are better than you really are; this is true conceit. But there are all kinds of conceit; for example, when you underestimate yourself, that, too, is conceit.

The fifth delusion is doubt. In this case, it is doubt about the Dharma —the Three Treasures, doubt about yourself, doubt about causation. The sixth delusion is called "wrong views." There are all kinds of wrong views that obscure wisdom. The last two among the delusions, doubt and wrong views, are actually the ones eliminated by having kensho. If your experience is clear enough, you will have a very good understanding and will no longer doubt.

In actual practice, delusions like greed, anger, ignorance, conceit, doubt, and wrong views are not only habitual, but exist in the emotional domain as well, and so are difficult to take care of. As with the five desires, it takes a long time to tame them. We will see in a later chapter how to practice right effort and how to pursue our practice. Our practice, our effort, and our wisdom take care of these delusions and desires little by little.

Discussion

Student: Telling someone to have few desires sounds straightforward enough, but I find it difficult to accomplish.

Glassman: The first thing I'd like to mention, which is true of all Eight Awarenesses, is their simplicity. Many things in Zen seem very esoteric or hard to grasp. There are either no words to express them, or the words we use are foreign to us. These Eight Awarenesses can usually be experienced easily. The words are simple. Interestingly, both Buddha's and Dogen Zenji's last talks are their simplest. They talk about such obvious things as what to do about desires, how to be satisfied, and how to enjoy serenity and tranquility. But in a way, that's the key. Just realizing and actually practicing these simple things is all that Zen is about. The problem is that it is hard to be so simple. It's hard to really make these things part of us, and so the practice becomes difficult. But once you've accomplished this practice, the things we're talking about become very simple.

Student: I desire to be better than I am. What's wrong with that?

Glassman: Whatever you have, that's what you have. You may say, "Well, why aren't I a foot taller than I am?" Because you're not. This is having a desire for something you are not, for things not already obtained. For instance, it's useless for you to want to be a foot taller. If we eliminate these unrealistic desires, then right here is nirvana.

Student: If nirvana is accepting myself just as I am, what is kensho?

Glassman: I want to differentiate between the first breakthrough, or kensho, and taming the body-mind. Deluded views and doubt are eliminated by what we call kensho, the enlightened state. Kensho is "seeing true nature," and when deep enough, is accompanied by the elimination of deluded views and of all doubt that you are the Three Treasures, that you are enlightened, that you are buddha. After kensho, the first four delusions—greed, anger, ignorance, and conceit—still remain.

This enlightenment experience culminates the first part of Zen training, the stage of "catching the bull" in the ten ox-herding pictures. Then we've got to tame the bull, and that takes twenty, thirty, forty years or more, depending on how ingrained and conditioned our body and memory are. This is a lifetime practice. People usually want somebody they think is well accomplished in Zen training to be perfect, to have no more greed, no more anger, no more ignorance, no more conceit. It doesn't work that way. Taming the body-mind is truly a lifetime process.

9: "Knowing How to Be Satisfied"

Dogen Zenji's Text

Second: *Knowing how to be satisfied:*
Knowing how much to take is called "knowing how to be satisfied."

The Buddha says: "You monks should contemplate knowing how to be satisfied if you wish to be liberated from suffering. The Dharma of knowing how to be satisfied is the realm of riches, comfort, peace, and tranquility. Those who know how to be satisfied are happy and comfortable even when sleeping on the ground. Those who do not know how to be satisfied are not satisfied even when dwelling in a heavenly palace. Those who do not know how to be satisfied are poor even though they are wealthy, while those who know how to be satisfied are wealthy even though they have little. Those who do not know how to be satisfied, and are always tempted by the five desires, are consoled by those who know how to be satisfied. This is called 'knowing how to be satisfied.'"

Maezumi Roshi's Commentary

As with the first awareness, it's very easy to understand the Buddha's words here. If we know how to be satisfied with the way we are right now, right here, that's all there is to know. This provides an interesting parallel to the awareness of "having few desires," which means that among those things we haven't yet obtained, we don't want much. Here

it says, "Knowing how to be satisfied with what we already have . . . ."
This is a wonderful power.

Ordinarily, we are dissatisfied with so many things. When we have
dissatisfactions, it can simply mean that we want more than we really
need. In one way or another, there is a way to be satisfied with what we
have. When we start wanting things, this wanting becomes endless and
it's impossible to satisfy ourselves. Then perhaps we come to the point
of asking, "If that's the case, what are we supposed to want?"

We gather to practice the Buddha Way together; that's a desire, isn't
it? We return to this phrase, "what we already have." We have a certain
amount already and there is also an appropriate amount to take. We use
oryoki, the eating bowls used in the formal Zen meals. Our oryoki are
considered as important as our life, as the Buddha's life itself. *O* means
"response"; *ryo,* "amount"; *ki* is "container." It's the container which
holds the amount necessary to respond to the need. All of us are *oryoki.*
All of us are containers which contain the necessary amount. Some containers are larger, some smaller. It's not a question of which is right or
wrong, better or worse. A large thing is a large thing; a small thing is a
small thing. That is to say, all of us are buddhas. When we understand
this, it is not a matter of being satisfied or dissatisfied. Our life is totally
sufficient. Becoming aware of this is wisdom.

"Knowing how to be satisfied" sounds a little negative, but it's not so
at all. Taking according to our capacity, according to the size of our
oryoki, is knowing how to be satisfied. On the one hand, if you have a
larger capacity and you take only a little bit of food, you won't be satisfied. On the other hand, if you take a lot of food and have a smaller
capacity, you'll also have a problem. You need to know how much to
take. Those who have a larger capacity should definitely take more.

What sort of measurement do we need to gauge our size? I remember that Sogaku Harada Roshi talked about the degree of aspiration of
our practice: what do we want and how much do we wish to accomplish?
This is a very good way to measure the size of your oryoki, of yourself.
Don't you think so? For those of you who have a profound, compassionate, devoted aspiration, even if you contain the whole world, you
may not be satisfied. Amitabha Buddha, the central Buddha in Pure Land
Buddhism, made forty-eight vows, and one of them was a vow to forego

his personal accomplishment until everybody is liberated. That's Amitabha's capacity, and certainly he's never been satisfied. Some people think that Buddhism is negative and passive, very unproductive, urging us to retreat to a mountain and meditate. But this is not true at all.

In any case, we have to begin from wherever we are, and wherever we stand, whatever capacity we have, we do our best practice. For example, if we are crippled and confined to our bed, then that's the only way we can practice at that point. That's how I understand "knowing how to be satisfied."

Now let's reflect upon ourselves again and upon how desires arise. Desires are one of the six delusions. In Buddhist psychology, consciousness is divided into eight different domains. The first five, the senses, are called pre-consciousness: eyes/sight, ears/hearing, nose/smell, tongue/taste, and body/touch. The most common desires have some connection with these five senses. The sixth domain is the consciousness which receives the images of sound, smell, taste, etc., and recognizes or perceives them. The seventh domain is called *mana*, the I-consciousness. For example, we see something and are attracted to it and want to possess it. What happens in that process is that first we perceive it, then we react to it as beautiful or ugly, pleasant or unpleasant. Discrimination of this kind carries us into the domain of the I-consciousness.

The eighth domain is called *alaya* or "storehouse" consciousness. The alaya consciousness is where everything, all memories, images, ideas, and information, is stored. On the one hand, it is deluded consciousness, the fundamental ignorance which prevents us from seeing the world as it is. And on the other hand, it is awareness, prajna wisdom itself, by which we can see that all phenomena are in themselves empty. Enlightenment turns that fundamental ignorance into prajna wisdom and allows us to see that from the very beginning, we are the buddha nature itself.

In order to be satisfied, we should thoroughly know ourselves as buddha nature itself, but until we really come to this point we can't be satisfied. Knowing ourselves thoroughly, even though our body, our existence, is finite—we can see that our life is nothing but the life of the whole world. We ourselves are the Dharma; we are already so. And as we live our lives, as we live the Dharma, we each consider how much we are supposed to take. We just know how to be satisfied. It's very simple and yet, if we think about it dualistically, it's not at all easy to be satisfied. In any case, the more we understand ourselves, the more we know how to be satisfied with our life.

Discussion

Glassman: "Knowing how to be satisfied" means using what we have in its best way. We're all dissatisfied in some way or other with something. Why are we dissatisfied?

Student: In trying to change my karma, I wasn't satisfied where I was, so I came here. Ideally, we should be satisfied with wherever we are, shouldn't we?

Glassman: On the other hand, it's all right to leave. Either way. If you stay it's fine; if you want to look for something, that's fine, too.

Student: What do we mean by "karma"?

Glassman: There are many ways that karma is interpreted in Buddhist texts. I think the most useful is the meaning of "what binds you, what's holding together your particular nexus of circumstances." Why am I here? Why am I related to this situation and these people? This teaches you how your mandala or matrix is and gives you a feeling of why it is and what you are. Your karma is what holds it together.

As I understand it, when you're in the realm of karma you're subject to cause and effect, and the enlightened person is one with cause and effect, whatever happens. In other words, as long as you think there is something wrong, you're bound. This doesn't mean you can't change or leave, but it's acceptance as opposed to resistance.

Student: Can you accept it and resist it at the same time?

Glassman : Sure.

Student: Sensei, how do you find it useful to look at karma in your life?

Glassman: In one sense, the very essence of life itself is what's meant by karma. In the most general sense, karma is what's happening. It's the very fact that things happen and cause other things to happen, and that all of those things manifest in the way that we perceive them right now. For instance, when people gather together to practice, there are many causes and effects that go into that. There is the fact that we've discovered practice and a place to practice. There is the fact that a seminar was set up. There's even the interest that made us want to look into Zen, into Buddhism, in the first place. There is the fact that this building was bought and this room was made into a seminar room. There are many causal chains, all manifesting themselves in the fact that we're talking here right now. All of that is what's called karma.

In a way, karma is just what's happening; there's nothing fixed. Somebody could get sick now or the room could collapse. Everything is constantly changing, and, in a broader sense, this change is called karma. Sometimes we look at ourselves and talk about personal karma. We start thinking: Why am I at the Zen Center? Why is my life the way it is? We look at our stream of life, and in trying to figure it out, we say it's our karma. But that gets a little tricky because then we're reducing it to a much smaller sphere, eliminating the biggest sphere of which we are also a part. If we look at it only in terms of "my" karma, we fall into the trap of getting stuck in our own ego, our own individuality. Karma is never that simple. We can't isolate ourselves, we've got to look at the whole because this whole is ourselves. This is why karma is difficult to pin down. To examine karma is to see beyond the notion of the small self and to see everything in its entirety. Then, seeing the whole, we need to see how everything interacts with everything else. This is how we develop a sense of karma.

But from our standpoint, the key is to realize that karma is ever-changing; it is never constant. It's completely opposite to the notion of possessions or fixed states of mind, and it's not some constant force that can lead us from one place to another. As soon as we see where we're at and pin it down to a certain state of mind, we're trying to regulate life, and all of a sudden we're stuck in our limited, conceptual thinking. This is when problems arise. Just accept the karma that is, accept life as it's flowing, and there can't be any problems. Just go along with it and do what you have to do, not trying to stop or fix life at some point, which simply can't be done.

Student: Does Buddhism ever use the words *fate* or *fated* or does it always just talk about karma? I think a lot of people use *karma* and *fate* synonymously.

Glassman: Fate to me has too strong a feeling, more deterministic. In Buddhism, both free will and determinism exist at the same time. You could say, "Because of what we do, we cause effects, we've got cause and effect going." But at the same time, we have free choice at any moment to do whatever we want. I think it was Rabbi Akiba, a famous Jewish sage, who said, "All is determined, but free will is given." Fate, I think, leaves out that complete freedom.

Student: I don't understand how I'm supposed to know what is the "right amount" of action to take.

Glassman: If we look at our own body, for example, the hand can pick up a lot of things. But if we try to pick up things with our foot, we have a harder time; it picks up much less. The two parts of the body have different potentials for carrying things, but that doesn't make one better than the other. It means they're different. Walking on the feet is much easier than walking on the hands. We tend to accept the limitations of the functioning of the parts of our body, yet we expect other people to be like us and to have our capacity for doing things. We don't accept the potential or the capacity of each person; we don't see what their container is. However, we should always look at these things in an active and a passive way. Being what we are, having the container we have, we should fully use our own potential. Then the question is, how do we determine that? When are we driving ourselves crazy by saying we should be doing more? When are we being too nonchalant by not doing enough? How do we figure out our own "size"?

Student: I struggled with that kind of question for months; nothing much came of it. Somewhere in my gut, I think I know. At the same time, I'm wondering, "Is this sufficient or not?" If there is even a question in my mind, the answer is already Mu. There seems to be a native wisdom in a person that says, "If you think that you might be tired, then you're tired. You know." The message has gotten through.

Glassman: How do you know your size?

Student: When I pant, I know I've had enough.

Glassman: But what happens if other people that are helping you are panting before you?

Student: You have to be sensitive to other people's feelings, but still, you have to leave it open to them to learn when they've had enough. You can't baby them, you can't always be concerned about whether they're stretching themselves a little too much. But if it's obvious that they're straining themselves, then you've got to help them out in some way.

Glassman: What gives me an uncomfortable feeling is that there is an implied separation in what you say between yourself and others. The mouth sees a lot of food, but the stomach can't eat it all. What is it that looks at food and says, "I want to eat more"? Eventually the stomach gets full, but the mouth says, "Oh, I'll have a pizza. I can get that one in, too." You know that the stomach is full, but you're saying, "Let the stomach worry about its problems. It's got to say something. It's got to throw up. I'll wait until I hear from it." Or perhaps you want to carry some load and your arms are getting tired, but you decide to wait until they collapse. If you're in the position of having people working with you, you've got to look at it not as "people working with me," but as "me working." You can't do more than "yourself," which includes all the people involved.

From my own experience, this feeling of knowing when to be satisfied or when not to be satisfied is really very strongly tied up with knowing our own capacity in its broadest sense. If we underestimate our capacity and stop too soon, we become dissatisfied. If we overestimate our capacity and do too much, we become dissatisfied. Underestimating leaves a feeling of, "Why aren't I doing enough?" Overestimating, "Why am I driving myself crazy and running myself down?" We must see our own capacity and our own potential. If we're aware of the fact that we're running ourselves down or that we're not doing enough, then that's one way of sizing ourselves, of seeing our capacity or our potential. Being aware of dissatisfaction can inform us about who we are, and where we're at, and make us more aware of all our dissatisfactions. For instance, if we're married, we can be aware of the satisfactions and dissatisfactions of husband and wife and kids as a family. We can be aware of the satisfactions and dissatisfactions of people working with us, and can see the capacity of that unit. We can enlarge our perspective even further, and become aware of the satisfactions, capacities, and potentials of everyone we come into contact with.

As our practice, zazen is the key to knowing our capacity, to knowing how to be satisfied. It's fascinating to see that based on each of these awarenesses, different schools and different methods have developed. In Zen, the emphasis is on the continual practice of zazen, allowing our head-tripping to slow down and these awarenesses to unfold naturally. Again, it's such a simple thing, but it's hard to do.

10: "Enjoying Serenity and Tranquility"

Dogen Zenji's Text

Third: *Enjoying serenity and tranquility:*
Being apart from all disturbances and dwelling alone in a quiet place is called "enjoying serenity and tranquility."

The Buddha says, "If you seek joy and peace in the serenity and tranquility of non-doing, you should keep away from disturbances and dwell alone in a quiet place. Those who dwell in quiet places are praised and respected by Sakrendra, chief of the gods, and by celestial beings. Therefore, casting away attachment to yourself-and-others, dwell alone in a quiet place and contemplate the cause of suffering. Those who crave the company of other people suffer from their relationship with them, just as a tree will be broken and die when too many birds roost in it. The bondage of worldly involvement will drown you in suffering, just as an old elephant drowns in the mud because he is unable to get out by himself. To liberate oneself from complicated involvements is called 'non-attachment.'"

Maezumi Roshi's Commentary

LET'S APPRECIATE the third of the Eight Awarenesses of the great person, "enjoying serenity and tranquility." In modern Japanese, the character *gyo*, which I translated as "enjoy," literally means "music." Etymologically it refers to the music of drums and strings, something we take pleasure in listening to. "To enjoy" is, for me, the implication of the word, so I translated it as "enjoying serenity and tranquility." Dogen Zenji defines this as, "Being apart from all disturbances and dwelling alone in a quiet place."

Taken literally, this passage means just what it says, but when we closely examine it, we find that it also means a good deal more. For example, "being apart from all disturbances"; where is there such a place? And what kind of "disturbances" do we have? "Dwell alone"— what does "alone" mean? What does "in a quiet place" mean? Buddha is speaking to his monks, but we can appreciate it as if he had said these words to all of us. "If you seek joy and peace in the serenity and tranquility of non-doing, you should keep away from disturbances and dwell alone in a quiet place."

We practice zazen; *za* means sitting, *zen* is derived from the Sanskrit term *dhyana*, which means "meditation." Making the mind quiet is *zen*. Making the body quiet is *za*, "sitting." The opposite of both is "running around." A spinning top provides an interesting analogy. When we don't spin it precisely, it wobbles and rolls around on the ground. But when we spin it right, it stays in one place and doesn't wobble. When we spin it really well, not only does the top stay in one place, but we can see the shape of the top as clearly as if it were standing still and not spinning. It doesn't mean that the top is not active. Our zazen is similar to that. Many people think that sitting is very inactive, a waste of time, but it is not so. Time-wasting occurs more often when we run around and exhaust our energies. In sitting, we raise our energy so that even our internal organs function more efficiently. Not surprisingly, in such an active, positive state, we enjoy serenity and tranquility.

If you seek joy and peace in the serenity and tranquility of non-doing . . . This "non-doing" is another key term. "Non-doing" doesn't mean "not doing anything." It means "doing something without being conscious of doing it, without being separated from the doing." Being one with whatever you do is non-doing.

Being "alone" means really being yourself, being serene and calm and undisturbed. Our life is all one life. This is the "alone," the "all one." If we could really be alone or all one, all our difficulties and problems would not disturb us. Instead, we would become even more courageous and determined to take care of these difficulties.

When we read a phrase like this, *Dwell alone in a quiet place . . .* , it seems to be telling us to go to the mountains and make ourselves quiet and peaceful. This is not how I understand it. I don't think it's really possible to escape to the mountains and become quiet. Can you do that? Probably you'd be more disturbed. When night came, wild animals would howl and the wind would whistle. During the day, even the wind blowing the leaves might disturb you. Not having a comfortable place to rest might disturb you. And what would you do for meals? That's not the way to "dwell alone in a quiet place." Rather, it's a matter of how to be calm and serene wherever we are.

There's a famous poem usually attributed to the Rinzai master Daito Kokushi, who, according to legend, lived for years with beggars under a bridge in Kyoto. "Doing zazen," he said, "I see the people on the Fourth and Fifth Street bridges like trees in a deep mountain." The Japanese used to wear wooden sandals, and when they walked on wooden bridges it made a racket. You can imagine how noisy it would be—horses going by, people crossing—and yet for him it was as quiet as living on a mountain. When we realize that everything is nothing but ourselves, then we can be thoroughly "alone."

Hakuun Yasutani Roshi gave me the name *Koun* when I received *inka* (seal of approval) from him. *Ko* means "alone," *un* is "cloud." *Hakuun* is "white cloud," and *Daiun*, the Dharma name of Yasutani Roshi's teacher Sogaku Harada Roshi, is "great cloud." *Koun*, "lone cloud." I really like that name; blown by the wind, everywhere it goes it's alone. No one can live your life for you. Your life is everything. Please appreciate this fact, this wonderful life. This is the Buddha Way.

Those who dwell in quiet places are praised and respected by Sakrendra, chief of the gods, and by celestial beings. All the gods and goddesses in heaven are going to praise you and respect your life. There's an interesting story about Yunju Daoying (J. Ungo Doyo), Master Dongshan Liangjie's successor (J. Tozan Ryokai), when he was practicing hard, doing zazen alone in the mountains. He used to come back to the monastery at a certain time of the day to eat, but suddenly he stopped coming. After a number of days, he finally showed up and Master Dongshan asked him, "Where were you? What happened to you?" Master Yunju explained, "Devas came down from heaven and offered me food, so I didn't need to come back." Master Dongshan scolded him, "I thought your practice was better than that. Devas brought food for you and praised your practice, but the fact that they recognized your goodness means that your practice is not quite good enough." Master Dongshan's rebuke is quite another way of regarding the praise of the gods, but here the Buddha says that if you practice well, that is, if you "dwell in a quiet place," even the gods will respect your practice and encourage you.

Therefore, casting away attachment to yourself-and-others, dwell alone in a quiet place and contemplate the cause of suffering. "Casting away attachment to yourself-and-others" sounds very passive and negative, but I don't think it is. We have very complicated human relationships, and good human relationships are crucial in order to make life smoother and more comfortable. In the family, community, workplace, and society at large, the most difficult task is always that of human relationships. You might think that difficulties arise because we all have different ideas or thoughts, but if human relations go well, all goes smoothly. Even in government, for example, among different political parties, if their personal relationships go smoothly despite different opinions or ideas, the government will function smoothly.

Casting away attachment to yourself-and-others, dwell alone in a quiet place. . . . Interestingly, Dogen Zenji actually uses the word "space" instead of "place": "quiet space." That quiet space could be any place. You can create quiet space in even the noisiest place. *Casting away attachment to yourself-and-others. . . .* When we stop making any distinctions between ourselves-and-others, attachment disappears. *And contemplate the cause of suffering. . . .* The causes of suffering always lie in the distinctions and discriminations one makes between oneself and others. This reminds me of a famous saying of the Buddha: "The three worlds are nothing but my possession, and all living beings are my children." Not only humans, but all living beings. This is being aware of the oneness of life.

> *Those who crave the company of other people suffer from their relationship with them, just as a tree will be broken and die when too many birds roost in it. The bondage of worldly involvement will drown you in suffering.*

Perhaps I have been emphasizing the original, intrinsic aspect a little too much. That is to say, all sentient beings are buddhas. But somehow until we become aware of it, we can't take this as fact. We have to realize it. Then we have to examine ourselves and experience it.

Sometimes students who come here are not satisfied with the practice and go somewhere else to practice. They return with all sorts of strong opinions, but with no way to resolve them and freely live their lives. We need to face ourselves directly—see where we stand, how much we can do, how to practice, and then integrate the many facets of ourselves in order to accomplish the Way—so that we can avoid unnecessary struggle and suffering.

The bondage of worldly involvement will drown you in suffering. Since Buddha here is talking just to monks, he uses the words "worldly involvement." But when we really appreciate the state of aloneness (all-one-ness), there is no distinction between aloneness and worldly involvement. Worldly involvement may not be the cause of disturbance in our life. However, if we are careless, it is like *an old elephant that drowns in the mud because he is unable to get out by himself.* When ten people get together, there are at least ten ideas and ten ideals, and if we are not strong enough, we'll be drawn this way and that way by the opinions and thoughts of others. Then we can't pursue our practice in an effective way.

To liberate oneself from complicated involvements is called nonattachment. Again, it sounds a little negative or passive, but by not getting entangled in disturbances, you see that you are the one who creates these disturbances. You can resolve them by realizing your own nature. Aloneness is nothing but "I." We can say, "I am alone (all-one) in the world," or we can say the "whole world is me," or "I am the whole world." Thus we can truly enjoy serenity and tranquility, since there are no disturbances. Isn't this nice?

Discussion

Glassman: "Being apart from all disturbances and dwelling alone in a quiet place is called 'enjoying serenity and tranquility.'" As Maezumi Roshi said, "dwelling alone" is the key. That is, if we are everything, that's aloneness or "all-one-ness." In Buddhism, when we talk about being alone, we mean that space in which we are everything. As Shakyamuni Buddha said, "Above the earth and below the heavens, I alone am the revered one." This "I" fills everything. If there is nothing outside of us, then how can there be disturbances? So through practice, let's experience this "dwelling alone!" Dwell alone here, now. Otherwise, wherever we go, it's noisy.

"Non-doing" is being one with whatever you are doing in this realm of aloneness, or "all-one-ness." In this state, the words *buddha* and *delusion* aren't necessary. In this state, the words *doing* and *non-doing* aren't necessary. It's just what you're doing. When we say, "I'm doing something," right there duality has arisen, it's not "alone." When this happens, we can't talk about "non-doing" because we've already dipped back into dualism.

Take swimming, for instance. When you become so good at swimming that you're no longer aware of swimming, then you are in the state of non-doing. Now perhaps it's extremely difficult to be apart from the sphere of all disturbances and to dwell alone. But in a way, this is zazen; this is our practice. Let's "dwell alone."

Student: Later in this passage, Buddha says, "Those who crave the company of other people suffer from their relationship with them. To liberate oneself from entangling involvements is called non-attachment." How is it possible to be in relation to other people without experiencing their suffering?

Glassman: When you dwell alone, when you're at one with with everything that's happening, that is the way to truly be with another. When you separate yourself from another, at that point you create the sphere of confusion and dualism. You're unclear about who you are. This distances you from what's happening. This is where the trouble comes in and what keeps you from truly being with another person.

Student: I'm not satisfied with that. What about the suffering part? If somebody is in pain and you're one with them, it's your pain too. Even if there is a slight distance between you, if you care something about them, you're going to be aware of pain.

Glassman: There's no reason why you shouldn't be. It's no different from being busy. Serenity and tranquility exist in the midst of busyness and pain—or sunshine and rain, or male and female, or hot and cold, or whatever the conditions are. That's just what's happening, and you deal with it as appropriately as you can. It's hard to accept that there isn't some trick for avoiding the "bad parts."

Student: It sounds like the Buddha is saying there's a way of getting out of experiencing suffering.

Glassman: When the Buddha says that the bondage of worldly involvement will drown you in suffering, it makes you want to hide away in order not to drown. The Buddha is speaking from a dualistic perspective. We've been talking about experiencing others' suffering. That's the realm of duality, of good and bad, up and down. The thrust of the Buddha's words is to transcend that duality, not by escaping but by putting ourselves totally into that involvement. When I hit you, what happens?

Student: It hurts.

Glassman: That's right. There is no one suffering; just this "it hurts." A lot of work has been done in recent years in hospitals, especially with people who are terminally ill with cancer and who are in chronic deep pain. The work, from a variety of approaches, centers on training the people to become one with their pain. These experiments have been very successful in that the people who have really involved themselves in the training generally die very differently from the people who have not been able to become one with their pain. It's apparently something that can be learned.

The key here is all-one-ness. Eliminate the distinction between yourself and others. At the moment of being hit, there is no suffering, there is not even knowing that you're hit. At that very moment, there's no distinction and there's no suffering. It doesn't mean that a rock doesn't land on your head really hard. Still, at that moment, that's all that there is; you don't think, "Oh, a rock came down and hit me on the head." It's just the pain, that sudden happening. In that state of oneness, it doesn't mean that you've rid yourself of the things you see and feel in a dualistic state. If you see a person on fire, you feel his suffering—he's burning up! But when there's really no separation between yourself and that suffering, there's no "you" left to suffer.

11: "Exerting Meticulous Effort"

Dogen Zenji's Text

Fourth: *Exerting meticulous effort:*
Exerting oneself meticulously and unceasingly in various bene-
ficial practices is called "meticulous effort." Be precise, not care-
less; go forward, do not regress.

The Buddha says, "If you monks exert meticulous effort,
nothing will be difficult to accomplish. Therefore, you should
make an effort to practice carefully, for when water flows constantly against a big rock, even a small amount of water will eventually wear a large hole. But if one who practices becomes lax, it
will be impossible to accomplish anything. It is like trying to start
a fire by rubbing two sticks together; if you stop rubbing before
the wood gets hot enough, you can't start a fire. This is what is
meant by 'meticulous effort.'"

Maezumi Roshi's Commentary

WHEN WE THINK ABOUT our practice and what is necessary for our
efforts to be meticulous, we find that just trying to be meticulous
is not sufficient. Right effort means effort channeled in the right direction. But since there are so many possibilities that seem "right" to us, it
is not often clear which direction is best.

Relatively speaking, all of us know what is good and what is bad. Yet,
in a way, it's ambiguous. A good thing for me to do isn't necessarily a
good thing for you, and vice versa. What is good or what is bad varies

with each one of us according to time, place, person, and circumstances. So, in terms of our practice, what is the right direction?

The most important key to our practice is our vows, our aspirations. Every day, we chant the Four Great Bodhisattva Vows. These are beautiful vows. As Buddhists, as people who practice in the enlightened way, every one of us is supposed to make these vows. The first vow is a vow to other people, to save or liberate all beings. The following three are to oneself: to have few desires; to master the Dharma; to realize the supreme Way. I want us to appreciate together the direction in which these vows point.

In order to discover your own direction, it is important to have great faith in yourself. Know that buddha nature and all kinds of virtues and wisdom are you yourself. See yourself as nothing but the very nature of being. Torei Zenji, a major Dharma successor of Hakuin Zenji, said that if you wish to realize the Way, you must first of all raise great faith. He then outlined ten stages of deepening faith, beginning with the faith that each one of us has the nature and boundless wisdom of all buddhas, and ending with the faith (which comes after one has accomplished the Way) in the importance of continuing and maintaining the Dharma in the future. Actually, though, the beginning and end of our practice is whether we really know ourselves as buddha. When you clearly realize this fact, you are truly enlightened. Then there is nothing but the sharing of your realization of yourself as buddha with other people. Unless you do this, you are not compassionate. Seeing yourself as buddha, believing and realizing this fact, you can't be anything but compassionate. So I really encourage you to have this strong, deep faith in yourself.

Having deep faith relates to koan study as well. Koan study is not playing with anecdotes or episodes that happened hundreds of years ago between masters and students. Right now, right here, we do koan practice in order to mature in the Dharma as ourselves; this is meticulous effort. Regardless of whether we are practicing with koans or not, in one way or another life itself is the koan. We are not studying the koan as such; we are always studying ourselves. Without the classical koans, we can practice quite well. Making right effort in shikantaza is still the same: have deep faith in yourself, and your zazen will be the zazen of the buddhas.

Consider the vows—what do we need to accomplish, and how do we accomplish it? First, raise the bodhi-mind, vow to accomplish *anuttara samyak sambodhi*, supreme, perfect enlightenment. Then practice right effort and realize what enlightenment is; realize who we truly are, our true nature. This is the state of nirvana. In this state, the vows are further nurtured. We continue to practice and deepen our realization. We attain nirvana, and again renew the vows to accomplish further. Dogen Zenji talks about endlessly accomplishing the Way. He compares our practice to a spiral, which doesn't necessarily have to be moving upward. We can enlarge ourselves in a horizontal way as well. By doing so, we share with more and more people the appreciation of this enlightened Way, the wonderful life of all of us together, which is nothing but each one of our lives. We must clarify our vows, then do our best. This is right effort.

The Eight Awarenesses themselves are meticulous effort. In the original Japanese, meticulous effort is *shojin*. *Sho* is literally "pure," or in Dogen Zenji's words, "being pure, it is not mixed." *Jin* is "progress," or as Dogen Zenji expresses it, "going forward, it does not regress!' This is right effort—just constantly keep on going.

The Buddha says that right effort is like a small amount of dripping water. When it drips continuously, eventually it wears a hole in stone. In another analogy, the Buddha compares right effort to making fire by rubbing two sticks together. If you stop before you get fire, regardless of how hard you try, you will never succeed. Our practice is the same. But after making a fire, what are we going to do? There are always further stages.

The Eight Awarenesses are very compelling: wanting little, we know how to be satisfied and enjoy serenity and tranquility. Then, with ever deepening satisfaction, contentment, and serenity, we endeavor to advance toward supreme enlightenment—not only by ourselves, but with everybody.

Discussion

Glassman: As Buddha says, if you keep rubbing two sticks together, eventually the fire will start. Our practice is as sure as this. This is consistency.

Student: What does consistency mean? What about all the doubts that go through my head, back and forth, back and forth, about wasting my time? Is that breaking the consistency?

Glassman: That's not breaking consistency. Being consistent is, for example, getting up every morning and sitting, then going to work and coming home, eating dinner with the family, then doing something at night. Doing that constantly, continuously, day after day, month after month, without deciding one day, "I'm not going to sit," and another day, "Today I'm going to sit all day." Just be consistent. When people ask me how much they should sit, I just say, "Pick a time, about fifteen or twenty minutes a day, but be consistent about it, and do that every day, five or six days a week. Don't sit one day for two or three hours and not sit for another week. Just be consistent, whatever your practice is.

It's important, however, to be consistent in the right direction. How do you know the right direction? You can feel it. In Buddhism, we talk about looking at four basic elements—time, place, person, and cir-cumstances—and realizing that those four elements are always chang-ing. But even having considered those four key factors, you just have to feel what the right direction is for you. And it's important to real-ize that what's right for you is not necessarily right for me. We're two different people. What's right to do in the library isn't necessarily right to do in the zendo; they're two different places. What's right to do now isn't necessarily right tonight when we're going to have a party; different places, different times. One person may like to sit for hours and hours, but that's not necessarily right for somebody who is just starting out and is going to be in pain. There is no standard which applies to everybody.

Student: In relation to consistency, doubt is a major hindrance for me. Whenever I doubt, it pulls me away from my practice.

Glassman: This doesn't necessarily mean you can't be consistent.

Student: Is doubt the same thing as lack of faith? This really con-cerns me.

Glassman: I think "faith" is a word that bothers people who are begin-ning practice. It brings up visions of believing in something whether you understand it or not. We talk about three major ingredients for practice:

great faith or trust, great doubt or inquiry, and great determination or perseverance. Those are the three qualities that Sogaku Harada Roshi mentioned as essential. If great faith is your strong point, then he suggested that your practice be shikantaza. Faith in what? Faith in yourself. Faith in the fact that, "Yes, I am buddha, I am the Three Treasures." Your questions are all resolved, because you've got this tremendous trust.

Now the second ingredient is great doubt or inquiry. "What is all this about? They're saying I'm buddha. I know I'm not buddha, but I want to be. I want to find out what this means." This great doubt drove Dogen Zenji. He wanted to know. All of the sutras (the recorded teachings of Shakyamuni Buddha) state that everyone is buddha, is buddha nature manifesting itself. But even Shakyamuni Buddha practiced for many years before he realized this. So we have this conflict: on the one hand we're buddha, and on the other hand we've got to practice to realize it. What does this mean? Shakyamuni himself had profound questions about life which drove him to practice.

We should be clear about the adjective *great* in the phrase *great faith*. "Great" describes the faith we have, that the lights will come on. We don't think, "I have this incredible faith thing going on with the electric company." We just flick on the switch, and we're surprised if the lights don't come on. Great faith is not incredible; it's everyday faith, only applied to a very fundamental issue instead of to something as superficial as an electric light switch. We're applying it to ourselves and saying, "I am the Way."

You don't have to make as much personal commitment to turning on the lights as you do to doing zazen. The initial years can be so much physical and mental agony. I've had important experiences in my practice, but they've faded, and I've never really understood what has kept me going. So I've been amazed to discover how much faith I have.

We don't need to tell ourselves that we're working all this hard for something that's really rare and elusive. We're working for something that is as common as dirt. Do I really think that by sitting here on this cushion every morning for five, ten, fifteen, or even twenty years, I'm going to be self-accepting and know who I am and my place in this world? There's no guarantee, but I'll never know if I don't try.

Student: You talked about great faith, doubt, and consistent practice. Can you also talk about drive?

Glassman: Actually drive is great determination. If we don't have the determination to resolve our questions about life, we'll just read some books and be satisfied. The reason we practice is because we have this determination to vindicate our faith and resolve our questions.

Student: I'm wondering whether it's possible that what Shakyamuni Buddha meant by practice is something much more general, much broader than merely sitting.

Glassman: Right. Zazen is the core of the practice, but that's not the only thing we do. Ours is a full practice. When we speak of Zen *practice*, it includes all of life.

Student: When you said, "Take what you can handle" in the discussion on "knowing how to be satisfied," could you also apply that to the kind of practice, as well as to the length of time you sit?

Glassman: I think so. I think there is another aspect to that too: take what you can handle and maybe just a little bit more. Push yourself a little bit; not unrealistically, but if you can sit easily for fifteen minutes a day, try twenty minutes. Give yourself a little nudge. My own feeling is that if you're consistent in your practice, one of two things will happen. Either it will turn out to be the wrong practice for you, or it will be the right one for you. Either way, you'll go on.

To get back to great faith, one of the ways of developing great faith is by studying ourselves. You know the famous words of Dogen Zenji, "To study the Buddha Way is to study the self. To study the self is to forget the self. To forget the self is to be enlightened by all things." Each one of us has a different capacity for faith, doubt, drive, and consistency. The deeper we go into ourselves, the more great faith naturally arises.

Let's remember these four aspects of practice: raising the bodhi-mind; practicing; attaining enlightenment, realizing the Supreme Way; then throwing away that realization, and beginning again. This defines "exerting meticulous effort." Doing this, we'll enjoy serenity and tranquility, even though everything is going on with all its goods and bads.

Student: Realizing and continuing, is that something like realizing the oneness, then seeing the differences?

Glassman: We're going to talk about oneness and differences a little later on, but in this case, it's just realizing anything, then throwing it away. Throwing one's realization away is at least as important as realizing it. Just keep going until you come to new insight, new realization, but don't stop; always throw it away and move on.

Student: When you throw it away, is that the same as forgetting it?

Glassman: Yes. Get rid of it; don't be attached to it. There is a specific kind of forgetting: not misplacing it, but making it so much a part of you that you no longer need to remember it.

It is also important in terms of meticulous effort to continually renew our vows as a way to raise the bodhi-mind. Every night, we chant: "Sentient beings are numberless, I vow to save them. Desires are inexhaustible, I vow to put an end to them. The Dharmas are boundless, I vow to master them. The Buddha Way is unsurpassable, I vow to attain it." When you really put yourself into these vows, you raise the bodhi-mind. Raising the bodhi-mind, you practice. And practicing, you realize. But don't stop there, throw it away and begin again. Right effort is encouraged by a group practice with a teacher who is capable of really teaching. It gives you something to check in with, to bounce off of, to get feedback from. "What needs particular attention at this point? Am I going on a tangent?" Then, you start to develop your own sense of when you are on course and when you're not.

12: "Not Forgetting Right Thought"

Dogen Zenji's Text

Fifth: *Not Forgetting Right Thought:*
This is also called "maintaining right thought." "Protecting the Dharma and not losing it" means "right thought," or "not forgetting right thought."

The Buddha says: "If you monks seek both a good teacher and good protection and support, nothing is better than 'not forgetting right thought.' For those who do not forget right thought, the thieving multitude of deluding passions cannot break in. For this reason, you should always keep right thought in your mind and regulate it well, for if you lose this thought, all sorts of merits and virtues will be lost. If the power of this thought is strong and firm, then even though you mingle with the thieving five desires, you will not be injured, just as, if you go into battle dressed in armor, you will not fear the enemy. This is the meaning of 'not forgetting right thought.'"

Maezumi Roshi's Commentary

IN JAPANESE, "not forgetting right thought" is *fumonen*, "do not forget the thought." For this *nen*, we use the English equivalent "thought." What is this thought? You might think that it is the same term as in the Heart Sutra, "Form is exactly emptiness, emptiness exactly form; feeling, thought, discriminatory awareness are likewise like this." But "right thought" is different.

More and more, I have become aware of how important words and expressions are. For example, Buddha says: if you really have right thought, it is like going into battle with armor. You can't get hurt. What kind of armor? What kind of battle? What kind of enemy is Buddha referring to? An analogy is always partial; we can't cover everything with an analogy. We should really understand what the Buddha is talking about as we practice the Buddha Way. Who has to wear such "protective armor," and from what must we protect ourselves?

We have to understand that there is no fundamental need to wear armor or to protect ourselves from anything. What is the armor? It's you! Each of us can be either indestructible armor or our own worst enemy. We could be animals, hungry ghosts, fighting spirits, buddhas, or bodhisattvas. "For this reason, you should always keep right thought in your mind and regulate it well."

If we take a step back and look at these teachings, we can see that they are also the Three Treasures, the very foundation of the Buddha Way. What are the Three Treasures? The Three Treasures are nothing but you! To really maintain and protect the Treasures is not forgetting right thought. Then everything else will follow quite naturally. Just be one with the Buddha, Dharma, and Sangha. In other words, be your true self.

Each of us has different characteristics and roles, and yet each of us is exactly the same. Each of us is the Buddha Tathagata. If you don't accept this, you are forgetting something; you are ignoring something; you are not maintaining right thought; you are not protecting right thought. When you truly maintain right thought, you are wearing the strongest armor, and you don't need to wear anything to protect yourself. Being yourself, just maintain this "not forgetting right thought."

In order to illustrate this point, let me again quote the famous koan about Yanyang and Zhaozhou. Yanyang asked Zhaozhou, "How about one who has nothing?" (Nothing to protect, nothing to wear, no enemy, no one to be harmed. Then what?) Zhaozhou said, "Cast it away." Yanyang asked further, "Having nothing, what is there to cast away?" Zhaozhou answered, "If so, carry it on." Reflecting upon ourselves, what is there to carry on, what is there to cast away? Again, I have to come back to the same point: we are the Three Treasures ourselves. Then being so, we know what to wear, what to protect, and what to cast away.

As I mentioned earlier, the word translated here as "thought" is *nen* in Japanese. The character *nen* consists of two parts: the top part means *ima*, "right now, at this very moment," and the bottom part is *shin*, "mind." The mind of this very moment, this is *nen*. Don't forget the mind of this very moment. Protect the mind of this very moment. Maintain the mind of this very moment. When we sit, what kind of mind do we have? Protect the mind of this moment and don't forget it.

There is a passage of the Avatamsaka Sutra: "The very beginning mind itself is the most accomplished mind of true enlightenment," or "The very moment of raising beginner's mind is the accomplishment of true awakening itself." We also have a common saying in Japanese: "Do not forget the beginner's mind." When we really understand this, beginner's mind is beginningless mind. Then we just maintain and protect it. Again, when we become aware that beginning is beginningless, in other words, the beginning is also the end and the end is the beginning. Without artificially trying to do anything, our life goes smoothly. This is not forgetting right thought.

Discussion

Glassman: Let me preface this discussion with a few words about the Three Treasures. As Maezumi Roshi has mentioned, "not forgetting right thought" means to remember that we are the Three Treasures. Twice a month, during the ceremony of atonement and renewing the vows *(fusatsu)*, we chant, "*Namo* Shakyamuni Buddha," which means, "Being one with Shakyamuni Buddha," or simply, "Be Shakyamuni Buddha." Be Manjusri Bodhisattva. Be Avalokitesvara Bodhisattva. Be one. In the jukai ceremony (receiving the precepts), the first thing we say is, "Be Buddha, be Dharma, be Sangha." These are our basic vows. But since we already are that, we are really saying, "Remember that we are the Three Treasures."

There are three ways of looking at the Three Treasures. The first is called the "Three Treasures of One Body." From this perspective, everything-as-it-is is the Three Treasures; there's no division. Everything is contained right here, right now: all space, all time. Everything is *just this*. The whole universe in space and time, all thoughts, actions, phenomena, everything going on is just this one body. If we look at it this way, then there's only one treasure, just this, and that's us. I am everything. Everything is nothing but me.

When we say "Three Treasures"—Buddha, Dharma, Sangha—we're looking at this one life from three perspectives. Buddha is unity, the fact that there is only one. Dharma is the multiplicity of phenomena, the fact that there are innumerable beings and things, and each one of them is unique. And Sangha is the harmony, the intimacy, the fact that unity and difference coexist without conflict. Altogether Buddha, Dharma, and Sangha are just different ways of talking about the one reality, which is nothing but ourselves, nothing but our life.

The second way of looking at the Three Treasures is called the Manifested Three Treasures. The One-Body Three Treasures must be realized. The historical Shakyamuni Buddha is a manifestation of this realization. His teachings are called the Dharma, and his disciples, the people studying with him, are called the Sangha. In this way, the Three Treasures are manifested in space and time.

The third way of looking at the Three Treasures is the Maintained or Abiding Three Treasures. All the enlightened teachers and their teachings that have been transmitted from generation to generation, and all of the practitioners down through the ages who gathered around them to study are the abiding Buddha, Dharma, and Sangha Treasures. Of course, this includes Maezumi Roshi and his Dharma successors, their teachings, and those who practice with them.

The primary implication of this fifth awareness, then, is to realize that our life is the Three Treasures and to live accordingly. The second implication of this awareness is that although zazen is the core of our practice, we have to manifest what we study. Some students may believe that there shouldn't be any study, that we just sit, but in fact there's a tremendous amount to learn. Having a firm foundation in the teachings, we practice without either forgetting or being attached to what we've learned.

Student: It really struck me when you said that if you wish for a good teacher, then consider "right thought." When I first met Maezumi Roshi, I remember how in his presence, I was aware of my busy mind. A good teacher is like that, really helping us to make "right thought" part of our total being, not just an intellectual concern.

Glassman: Definitely, that's true, and Shakyamuni Buddha is also saying a little more than that. He's saying that if you want to practice, if you want a good teacher, if you're looking for protection and support, nothing can be more essential than remembering that you are the Three Treasures.

Student: What is this remembering? It's not just intellectual—isn't it remembering with our total being?

It seems that we're talking about being mindful, completely one with what's happening at the moment, so that there's no separation between us and it. Am I right about this?

Glassman: Fumonen is translated as "not forgetting right thought." My understanding of the word *nen* is that it's not only mindfulness as you described it, but it also has the connotation of remembrance, of knowing something and not forgetting it. In the Ten Grave Precepts, the last precept is: Do not speak ill of the Three Treasures. The implication of this precept is that if you forget that you are nothing but the Three Treasures, then you are speaking ill of the Three Treasures.

We also talk about defiling the precepts and breaking the precepts. These two must be distinguished. We defile the precepts at every moment. For example, the first precept, "Do not kill," applies to everything: insects, plants, bacteria, or any life. Every time we breathe, eat, wear clothes, or take a step, microorganisms die. We are constantly killing, yet we vow not to kill. In reality we defile all of the precepts at every moment, and we need to appreciate this fact. It's like dirtying the dishes—we use them, and so we must constantly clean them. This is defiling the precepts.

However, when we break the precepts, we renounce the Three Treasures. This is not just to think that we're not doing so well, but rather to completely lose faith in the value of our lives. To extend the dishes analogy, this would be breaking the dishes. Dogen Zenji says, "If the power of this right thought is strong and firm, then even though you mingle with the thieving five desires, you will not be injured."

The basis of great enlightenment is to know you are the Three Treasures. It's very easy to use statements such as "everything is as it is" to justify an "anything goes" attitude. Beat Zen developed on this very idea—if we are mindful and if we are one with this very moment, then there's no problem. But there's more to it than that. We must realize and never forget that we are the Three Treasures, and let this be the basis for our actions. This is not an idea that we're attached to, but rather it's ingrained in us that we are the Three Treasures. Then being one with this moment, we move in the right direction.

Maezumi Roshi compared faith to a steering wheel. He said that if we don't have a steering wheel and we just put our foot on the gas pedal of determination, we'll lurch ahead blindly and bang into all sorts of things. But by maintaining right thought, thoroughly remembering that we are the Three Treasures, we'll go in the right direction.

Student: Several weeks ago I was reading about this "not forgetting right thought" and felt very much at one with the ideas expressed. Then, for the last two weeks, I've been involved in a very difficult work situation and have been wallowing in a lot of negative feelings. Just before coming to the zendo tonight, I was reminded that the discussion was going to be about "not forgetting right thought," about not forgetting that I am the Three Treasures, and I realized that that's exactly what I had been doing. By forgetting, I was robbing myself by a desire for money, material things, and fame. Now I'm being reminded that I am the Buddha, Dharma, and Sangha. From my experience, forgetting that can be very messy.

Glassman: We have to know what it means when we say that we are the Buddha, Dharma, and Sangha. It doesn't matter if Shakyamuni Buddha or Dogen Zenji, or even you yourself is saying so, it won't mean a thing if you don't realize what this means. And once you do, you won't forget it.

There are degrees of understanding. Each one of us has some idea of what it means to be the Three Treasures, and yet nobody really knows it completely. In fact, "What are Buddha, Dharma, and Sangha?" is a lifetime question for us all.

13: "Practicing Samadhi"

Dogen Zenji's Text

Sixth: *Practicing Samadhi:*
Dwelling in the Dharma undisturbed is what is called "samadhi."

The Buddha says: "When you monks unify your minds, the mind is in samadhi. Since the mind is in samadhi, you know the characteristics of the creation and destruction of the various phenomena in the world. For this reason, you should constantly practice with diligence and cultivate all kinds of samadhi. When you gain samadhi, the mind is not scattered, just as those who protect themselves from floods guard the levee. This is also true for practice. For the sake of the 'water of wisdom,' then, cultivate samadhi well, and do not let it leak. This is called 'samadhi.'"

Maezumi Roshi's Commentary

IN THIS PASSAGE, Dogen Zenji is using the term *zenjo*. Originally, the word *zen* came from the Sanskrit *dhyana*, which was phonetically rendered into Chinese as *ch'anna*, and eventually shortened to *ch'an* (J. *zen*). *Dhyana* originally meant "quiet thinking" or "contemplation." By contemplating certain objects or subjects, one learned to concentrate. Samadhi (J. *jo*) is the state of absorption itself, the state in which subject and object are one. In the Eight Awarenesses, practicing dhyana or samadhi is the sixth. In the Indian tradition, various degrees of samadhi were identified. Buddha is saying here that you should practice different kinds of samadhi.

In our daily life, we frequently experience samadhi, the state of becoming one. We can observe samadhi in our work, study, watching television, or thinking. There is even the samadhi of gambling. It's rather easy to get into the kind of samadhi where we are absorbed in whatever we are doing. We call this "samadhi in the realm of desire." We speak of three worlds—the realms of desire, form, and no-form. These worlds are not geographical or spatial; they exist in the mind. In the Diamond Sutra, it says that the three worlds are created by the mind.

What states of mind are these? The realm of desire is the usual state of mind in which we live. We relate to the external world under the influence of conditioning created by our senses and awareness. When we see something, we are conditioned by what we see. Our hearing, smelling, tasting, touching, and awareness function in the same way. We are very easily conditioned by thinking, and so create all kinds of problems and frustrations. Strictly speaking, we don't call these conditioned states "samadhi," even though they are concentrated states, such as in forgetting ourselves while absorbed in a movie.

In the realm of form, strong attachment to the senses and awareness disappears. I don't know whether it's correct to explain it in this way, but you become more genuinely spiritual, yet you are still attached to the existence of certain objects, though in a much more subtle way.

The third realm, the realm of no-form, is still more subtle and is subdivided into four different stages. Samadhi in the realms of form and no-form is called "fundamental samadhi." This is the samadhi we are in when we are genuinely practicing, when we can sit and concentrate well. Beyond that, there is one more state of samadhi which is called "the samadhi of no leaking." In this state, not even the slightest attachment to any thought remains. These are very technical descriptions and may not be especially helpful in the context of practice. But, we should be aware that there are many different levels and kinds of samadhi.

In Zen practice, what kind of samadhi should we develop? The Chinese sometimes translated the Sanskrit word *samadhi* as *cheng shou* (J. *sho ju*), literally "right receiving." By concentrating well, we still the waves of the mind and are able to see things as they are. The waves are caused by the wind of thoughts and ideas. Of course, there is nothing wrong with this wind, but when we are blown about by it, it causes difficulties. The practice of samadhi eventually cuts the source of this wind.

Perceiving externals as they are, we naturally know how to respond to situations. This is "right wisdom," which flows spontaneously out of deep samadhi. As the Sixth Ancestor Huineng says in the Platform Sutra, "Samadhi itself is the substance of wisdom; wisdom itself is the functioning of samadhi."

Unfortunately, our samadhi power is rarely this good. In our practice, we experience many degrees of absorption which we also call samadhi. In this sense, we can say that samadhi is the state of mind prior to wisdom. We can progressively increase our samadhi power, and then any chance happening can make us aware of our wisdom. As a matter of fact, we are using this wisdom all the time, but we are just unaware of it.

We often experience ourselves as separate from all else. This is the attachment to one's identity—"I am different from anybody else, anything else." All kinds of subject-object relationships are established. Not only human relationships, but relationships to everything. We say, "This is mine; that's yours." Or "That's none of your business; it's my business." Or "I think such and such. I am right, you are wrong." Buddha says such upside-down thinking is a delusion, but we believe that what we think is right.

Right wisdom is the vision with which we see equality or oneness. This is the beginning of acquiring wisdom in a different dimension. The enlightenment experience is nothing but awakening to this wisdom, and samadhi makes it possible. In deep samadhi, the subject-object relationship is eliminated, and we realize this non-dual wisdom. For example, if we take a magnifying glass and use it to focus sunlight on a piece of paper, eventually the paper will burst into flame. When we don't focus those rays properly, no matter how long we hold the magnifying glass, the paper won't burn. The same is true of our practice. We can practice zazen for many years, but without strong concentration, our samadhi will not come to fruition in the experience of enlightenment.

At the Zen Center of Los Angeles, our practice generally takes three different forms: awareness of breathing, koan study, shikantaza. There are many ways to practice. Even within koan practice itself, there are many koans. Whatever problem or difficulty we are facing can be a wonderful koan. Or we can practice by concentrating on a particular object. Depending on the person, certain types of concentration are recommended. For example, concentration on breathing is a very effective practice. It is not necessarily only for beginners. By following, counting, or noting the breath, we can create deep samadhi.

The proper posture of the body is important for good sitting. If you sit with your chest compressed, you can't breathe well. So when you sit, the chest should be open. Sit upright, and you can naturally breathe more deeply and easily. Those who are doing koan practice must let the mind be saturated with the koan. Then concentrate and go into samadhi. Koan is mind. The same is true for shikantaza. We train ourselves in this way, and when the time ripens, the flower of wisdom opens.

Therefore, when you sit, please sit well and don't scatter your attention. Whatever disturbs your concentration is makyo, and there are all kinds of makyo (see glossary). One kind of makyo is scattered, busy mind. Another is dull, drowsy mind. When you sit, you should avoid these two major tendencies. Sit well and don't leak your samadhi. As Buddha says, "For the sake of the 'water of wisdom,' cultivate samadhi well and do not let it leak out." Regardless of whether you are aware of it or not, you are the container of wisdom. Don't let it leak. Take care and preserve your samadhi well. Then, when the time comes, you'll really see how to utilize this wisdom fully, not only for yourself, but for other people as well.

Discussion

Glassman: Most people who talk to me about samadhi think of it in only one sense, that is, as very deep concentration. I remember one sesshin I attended where a woman entered that kind of samadhi. It was the first time I had ever seen anyone go into "deep samadhi." She hadn't been practicing for very long, and this was perhaps her second or third sesshin. When she didn't get up at the end of the first sitting in the afternoon, Roshi asked me to let her be, and we intentionally avoided disturbing her during walking meditation. She ended up sitting about five or six hours, through dinner and break, and then, towards the end of the evening sitting, she heard the dokusan bell and got up and went to dokusan. She had no idea how long she had been sitting, and she had no pain in her legs. She just stood up and went to dokusan as if she'd been sitting for half an hour.

Such samadhi is what people generally think of when they hear the term *samadhi*. In our sitting, as we drop our attachment to our desires, we enter into samadhi in the realm of form. Our sitting deepens to the point where we're not distracted by or attached to sensory impressions. It doesn't mean they're not there. We're still aware of ourselves and of those things, so there's something of a split between ourselves and so-called externals.

But then our sitting goes even deeper, to the point where not only isn't there any attachment, but there's no division at all. A bell sounds; it's just the bell. No "I" exists, nothing separate. There's a story of one roshi who screamed out in pain when the bell was struck. He had become the bell itself. And then there's the story of the monk who was doing zazen in an inn, working on the koan "the cypress tree in the garden." When a thief slipped in through the window, the thief shouted out in alarm and jumped back out the window. All he saw was a cypress tree in the middle of the room! This is called the samadhi of no-form. The monk wasn't there anymore, only the tree. This is what Dogen Zenji is referring to when he says: "For the sake of the 'water of wisdom,' cultivate samadhi well and do not let it leak out."

Any kind of attachment, any kind of separation or clinging, no matter how small, is the leaking of samadhi, the leaking of the water of wisdom. "No leak" means that not even the slightest attachment to anything remains. If the monk was aware of being the cypress tree, then his samadhi leaked. This state of "no leak" is difficult to attain, and in our koan study, we're asked to present the koan with that spirit. In any case, as we sit, our concentration becomes stronger and stronger, the gap between subject and object becomes less and less, and we experience different levels of samadhi. Yasutani Roshi says that after sitting twenty years you can finally say that you've begun to learn how to sit, and that your samadhi has matured. Many of us will take even longer than that. In a broader sense, whatever state of mind we're in at any particular moment is our samadhi at that time.

There's a famous koan in which a monk asks Yunmen, "Tell me, what is samadhi?" And Yunmen says, "It's rice in the bucket." That is, it's everything that happens during the day—eating rice, cooking meals, driving the car, sweeping the floor. Please don't worry about what level of samadhi you're experiencing. What's much more important is constant practice.

Student: Could you talk about the relationship between wisdom and samadhi and also the relationship between deep samadhi and enlightenment?

Glassman: It can be said that each aspect or our practice is the functioning of another. For example, the lighted candle is samadhi; the light it gives off is the functioning of its wisdom. But you can't differentiate between them. There's just the candle burning and giving off light. The light is the functioning of the candle. Wisdom in Buddhism has nothing to do with knowledge or intelligence—wisdom is simply the functioning of what is.

Student: But then what about prajna wisdom? Is that a different kind of wisdom, or is it wisdom in the broadest sense? And then is it an expression of a functioning of a particular kind of samadhi?

Glassman: Just as there are many degrees of samadhi, so there are many kinds of wisdom. We talk about prajna wisdom, which we sometimes call the wisdom of emptiness. This is the wisdom of seeing the oneness of all things, which is the wisdom of deep samadhi. On the other hand, if my samadhi is weak and I'm attached to lots of different things, then that's the kind of wisdom that will emerge. We have difficulty because we want to think that wisdom is somehow different from our normal, everyday functioning. But the statement "Everything as it is, is buddha nature" means exactly that. Even the state of clinging to things is buddha nature, and the functioning of that state is wisdom. Enlightenment is just the experience of realizing this fact. In a way, it's a very simple fact, but we don't want to accept it. Somehow we expect wisdom or buddha nature to be something special, something more.

As for the relationship between samadhi and enlightenment, we say that the depth of enlightenment depends on the depth of samadhi. This is only natural. Usually, we have a first opening early in our practice, when our samadhi is not that deep. Then we study koans to clarify and polish that first insight, until at some point we have another, much deeper realization. We then no longer have any doubt about why we practice, or what direction our practice should take. But even at this point, if we stop practicing, our realization will fade and our samadhi will leak away.

Samadhi is like a reservoir. When we sit, we're filling the reservoir, and as the reservoir gets fuller, we become more stable and more able to live our lives with confidence. Naturally insights will arise, and we let those insights go and continue our practice. Otherwise, we become attached to our realizations and our samadhi dissipates.

Student: Many arts, particularly the martial arts, center on cultivating *joriki,* the "power of samadhi." In tai ch'i or aikido, for example, this flow of energy is called ki (Ch. ch'i), and it is very important to develop and use it. How is Zen practice different from these practices?

Glassman: We call people who practice in this way joriki junkies, or samadhi freaks. They appear in Zen practice, too. Zen practice is essentially letting go and going on. This doesn't mean we don't generate deep samadhi, but that's not our emphasis. It's a byproduct. We don't stop at any particular inn, for example, the joriki inn. Our goal, if any, is to be completely free. This means that as we develop our samadhi and use it, we have to let go of our attachment and go beyond it. Again, if our powers of concentration are only available for one particular art or discipline, this is not Zen samadhi. In Zen, our samadhi power should function twenty-four hours a day, everyday throughout our life.

Student: When I started practicing, I could see that my ability to relate to people or situations seemed to relate directly to the quality of my samadhi. When I'd reach a barrier, I'd always feel that it was something in my sitting, and I'd try to resolve it by sitting more. It was a very different experience when I tried to resolve the barrier by just staying and working with the situation, letting go of the idea that the best way to resolve it was to increase my samadhi.

Glassman: I think this is true. What's also important is to practice consistently so that our samadhi, our stability, just keeps steadily improving. I often hear people say, "I used to sit really strong. I had tremendous samadhi and now nothing seems to work right." But these same people are the ones of whom you'd say, "Their practice has become so solid over these past few years." When we look at ourselves, we can't see ourselves over the span of a few years. We are only aware of our faults and think, "I should be doing so much better." In fact, the stronger our sitting becomes, the more clearly we see the weaknesses and limitations of our practice. It's an endless process. And the key is just to sit consistently, and little by little our concentration will develop, our samadhi will deepen, and our joriki and stability will increase.

Student: What's the relationship between different practices such as shikantaza or the koan Mu or koan practice and different kinds of samadhi?

Glassman: Certain koans, like "the cypress tree in the garden" or "Mu," are very similar to shikantaza and following the breath in the kind of samadhi that is developed. Then there are other koans which aren't oriented that way at all, which are more concerned with improving the way we express our understanding.

Student: So a practice that emphasizes shikantaza or breathing would be a practice which emphasizes samadhi?

Glassman: Yes. Koan study is a mixture, whereas these other practices more directly emphasize building samadhi. Ultimately, however, the difference is one of emphasis.

In twelfth-century China, there was an ongoing debate between the "silent illumination" style of Zen, headed by Master Hongzhi Zengjue (J. Tendo Shogaku), and the koan style, headed by Master Dahui Zonggao (J. Daie Soko). The former stressed samadhi, while the latter emphasized insight or satori, realization. The arguments on both sides were often quite heated. Yet when he died, Hongzhi named Dahui to succeed him as head of his monastery. The differences between the two teachers never obscured the basic realization which they shared.

14: "Cultivating Wisdom"

Dogen Zenji's Text

Seventh: *Cultivating wisdom:*
Wisdom is aroused by hearing, reflecting, practicing, and realizing.

The Buddha says: "When you monks have wisdom, you are without greed. Always reflect upon yourselves; do not lose this wisdom. In this way, you can attain liberation in my Dharma. One who does not is neither a follower of the Way as a monk or layperson, nor is there any other name for such a one. True wisdom is a stout boat which crosses the sea of old age, sickness, and death; it is also a great bright torch in pitch black ignorance; a good medicine for all sick people; a sharp axe which fells the tree of delusion. Therefore, by means of this wisdom which is heard, reflected upon, and practiced, you will increase your merit. When one has the illumination of wisdom, even though one's eyes are merely physical eyes, one is a 'clear-seeing person.' This is what is meant by 'wisdom.'"

Maezumi Roshi's Commentary

THE BUDDHA SPEAKS of wisdom in plain, simple words using analogies. He says, "When you have wisdom, you are without greed." We suffer because our desires are not fulfilled, and greed occurs because of ignorance. From a Buddhist point of view, there are three poisons which disturb us: greed, anger, and ignorance. When we examine these three poisons, each of them can be traced to ignorance. Because of our ignorance, we experience anger or aggression and greed, which are the opposites of compassion and generosity. In this awareness, the Buddha talks about how we can turn this ignorance into wisdom by hearing, reflecting, practicing, and realizing.

Briefly speaking, there are two kinds of wisdom: partial and complete. Complete wisdom manifests in enlightenment. In partial wisdom, there are four modes, three of which are mentioned here: the wisdoms of listening; reflecting; practicing. There is also a fourth innate wisdom. For instance, we instinctively know how nurse at our mother's breast.

Through the wisdom of listening, we can understand the nature of life. When listening to others, we hear them against the background of our own opinions or criticism, which decreases the effectiveness of listening. When we listen, just really listen, being one with whatever is said. In this way, we direct ourselves toward the supreme enlightenment, which is anuttara samyak sambodhi.

After listening, we should carefully consider what we have heard or read. But just thinking is not enough, regardless of how well we think, or how good our ideas are. Then comes practice, which is wisdom itself. However, just practicing is still not yet complete wisdom. All these are still forms of partial wisdom. By personally realizing what Buddha says, it becomes complete wisdom.

This awakening is unique to Buddhism. Many people seem to depend on an external figure or idea, but there is no external in Buddhism. Recall the famous expression, "When you meet the Buddha, kill the Buddha. When you meet the ancestors, kill them." We don't recognize any external creator. To become awakened, to become aware of the true face of life, is Buddhism. Then what we find is not at all difficult to explain. As I always say, enter the sphere of oneness, find out that there is no division between ourselves and externals. To actually see this is wisdom.

According to another Buddhist teaching, there are four kinds of wisdom: great, mirror-like wisdom; the wisdom of equality; the wisdom of subtle observation; and the wisdom of the senses, which in our daily life we are using from morning to night. As I mentioned in the chapter on the second awareness, in Buddhist psychology our consciousness can be examined on eight different levels. The first six are the senses, which in

Buddhism include conscious awareness. The seventh level is *mana* consciousness; the eighth is *alaya* consciousness. The five preconsciousnesses, the senses, function as the wisdom of seeing, hearing, smelling, tasting, and touching. The sixth consciousness functions as the wisdom of subtle observation, the seventh as the wisdom of equality, and the eighth as mirror-like wisdom.

Somehow in our life, these wonderful consciousnesses often do not function as wisdom. We don't see all as one; we separate externals and ourselves by having the idea or thought of "I." "I am something different from you. I am not this paper. I am not a buddha. I am not the sun. I am not a tree." But what is "I," this self-referencing I-consciousness? It's what we call mana consciousness, the seventh consciousness. Actually, this "I" doesn't really exist, but somehow we firmly believe that it does, which is the very cause of our problem. In our practice, we cut off this false, deluded idea of "I." Dogen Zenji says in the *Shobogenzo Genjokoan:* "To study the self is to forget the self. To forget the self is to be enlightened by all things." What happens when we forget the self? We are enlightened by all things; we have become one with everything. Being so, we realize the wisdom of equality. We see the universal nature of all of everything—this is kensho.

We can see this universal nature from an entirely different perspective. No two things are exactly the same; everything is different, and we appreciate all phases of life. Even two seemingly identical, blank pieces of paper are totally different. Even two specks of dust are totally different. When we see these differences, this is the wisdom of subtle observation.

When we see that sameness is nothing but difference, and difference is nothing but sameness, that one is all and all is one, this is the great, round, mirror-like wisdom. Then whatever we see, whatever we do, becomes the expression of wisdom. This is called the wisdom of communication with so-called externals, or the wisdom of the senses. Having such wisdom, we can go on with life regardless of whatever hardships we encounter. In the text, Buddha says:

Always reflect upon yourselves; do not lose this wisdom. In this way, you can attain liberation in my Dharma.

In its largest sense, dharma refers to all phenomena. In its narrowest sense, Dharma can be understood as the teachings of the Buddha. Among these teachings, the Buddha expounded the law of causation, the causes by which we will attain supreme enlightenment. Certain causes brought each of us to this life that we are living now. All is causation; this is one aspect of Dharma.

Another important aspect of Dharma is that it is completely empty—everything has no fixed substance. If we think of ourselves, there is no such thing as "I," no human essence, no object essence, no fixed substance or entity. All is constantly changing.

One of the four vows we chant each evening is, "The Dharmas are boundless, I vow to master them." To see clearly that the Dharmas are boundless, and to continue practicing to master these Dharmas, is wisdom. Again, returning to the text:

One who does not is neither a follower of the Way as a monk or layperson, nor is there any other name for such a one. True wisdom is a stout boat which crosses the sea of old age, sickness, and death; it is also a great bright torch in pitch black ignorance; a good medicine for all sick people.

In a way, the Buddha's teachings are like medicine. Good doctors are the ones who really know precisely what the sickness is and can prescribe the most effective medicine in the appropriate amount. Recovery is then fast. As a matter of fact, there are four different ways that Buddha expounded the teachings. One way is very general: what he said is true for everybody. Secondly, he taught according to the needs of each particular individual. The third way literally means "the teaching of giving medicine." Knowing the precise cause of suffering, Buddha taught the remedy for it. Then the fourth way is the essential truth beyond all skillful means. The Buddha spent all his life expounding the Dharma, but waited over forty years before teaching emptiness, the first principle of essential truth.

Like the Buddha, we must have patience and diligence in following the Way. In fact, such patient practice itself is wisdom. When the time comes, the flower of enlightenment will bloom, and yet that is not the end. Our practice continues forever. It's all medicine. Let's continue to take that medicine and diligently cultivate wisdom together.

Discussion

Student: Would you consider our preconceived ideas and value judgments as a part of I-consciousness?

Glassman: Yes, all the opinions and ideas that we have which make us separate from others are part of what we define as "I." If we didn't have any of those, then it would be very hard to find this "I."

Student: When a person is in deep samadhi and doesn't realize that she is sitting there, which consciousness is she in at that point? Is it mirror consciousness or pure consciousness?

Glassman: It could be mirror wisdom, but it could also be just a state of dullness. It really depends on the functioning as to whether it is wisdom or whether it's simply a kind of dull state.

The Sixth Ancestor said that samadhi and prajna are not two different things. The deeper our samadhi in sitting, the closer we get to just washing the dishes or just scratching our nose. Life is an unending samadhi, so in sitting, any of these wisdoms can manifest. In our actions, any degree of samadhi can also manifest.

I think we must realize Shakyamuni's declaration upon awakening, "How wonderful, how wonderful, all sentient beings have the wisdom and virtue of the fully enlightened one." That is, pure wisdom is how we're functioning, how the senses are functioning. We eat, sleep, sit zazen, do all kinds of things. We talk about these stages of samadhi as ways of looking at the practice, but, what's the difference between our functioning and the Buddha's functioning? When we say there is none, this is not entirely accurate. But if you say there are differences, then what are they?

Student: I get into two kinds of samadhi. In one, I tend toward shikantaza and become very aware of everything. Hopefully, there is nothing that gets by, at least for a short period of time. The other kind of samadhi is where the sensory world begins to fade and keeps moving further and further away. These two states seem to be totally different. Can you comment on this?

Glassman: My understanding of Zen practice is that it should be the first kind; one should become really aware.

Student: I don't necessarily choose the second, but sometimes I can be trying so hard to maintain this alertness and before I know it, it's slipped away. Is this bad sitting?

Glassman: No. You know how to sit, and it's not necessary to be constantly questioning or worrying about how your sitting is going. I know for myself that, when I sit, each time is different, each day is different. When I sit, I just sit; it goes however it goes. To try to figure out whether it was a good sitting or bad sitting, or the right way or the wrong way, isn't really the point. I think if you keep sitting and are consistent, you need not worry about whether it's right or wrong or good or bad. Your sitting will just naturally deepen.

Student: I'd like to comment on wisdom and patience being the same, and then your later statement that everything we do is wisdom. I don't feel that when I'm being impatient, I'm being wise.

Glassman: When you say that, though, you're using the word *wise* in the way we use the word *smart.* Wisdom is not that kind of thing.

Student: Am I in a state of wisdom when I'm being impatient?

Glassman: Prajna wisdom is seeing things as they are, and the functioning of wisdom, therefore, is the functioning of things as they are. So you could say that being impatient is nothing but the functioning of wisdom. Prajna wisdom is nothing but seeing and realizing that things are as they are and are functioning in that way. We're using this wisdom all the time. Sitting is the functioning of wisdom. Throwing up is the functioning of wisdom. It's got nothing to do with being smart or dumb. Dumbness itself is the functioning of wisdom. But I didn't answer your question. How is wisdom the same as patience?

What strikes me is that as long as I separate myself from what's happening, then I can't really be patient. I can force myself to keep quiet, but I can't really be patient. As soon as I can simply be one with what is going on, then there is no need for patience. Patience is simply an essential part of what's happening. Of course, this is also the same as the wisdom of equality. So this is the starting point of patience.

Another name for Shakyamuni Buddha is "He who is able to be patient." The wisdom of subtle observation, of seeing the differences, is seeing the fact that things are going at their own pace and are happening the way they have to happen. For example, we can't expect a tortoise to be running at the speed of a greyhound, but if we make the mistake of thinking all things are the same, then we may ask, "Why isn't the tortoise running like a greyhound?" Different people have different capacities. If we really see these differences, this is patience. But if we have some idea of how they should be and expect them to be other than they are, this is the opposite of wisdom and this is when impatience arises. We're impatient because we don't accept differences.

Similarly, we're impatient with ourselves because we can't acknowledge that our pace is different from somebody else's pace, our capacity is different from somebody else's. We may think, "I want my zazen to be free of thoughts," and so we get impatient. But subtle observation is seeing, "This is how I am." Seeing that, we just sit, just act, and this becomes pure wisdom, or functioning wisdom.

Student: If each consciousness contains all of the eight consciousnesses, then how are the six senses contained in the alaya consciousness?

Glassman: Can you show me a place where one of these eight levels of consciousness exists by itself? For example, can the *I*-consciousness be isolated from the other seven and function by itself? What are we describing? Dogen Zenji says, "To study the Buddha Way is to study the self." We're studying the self, so we really can't separate these eight consciousnesses. We can talk about them separately, in just the same way that we can talk about different parts of speech, if we want to diagram a sentence. It's an expedient means. Categorizing has meaning and value, but ultimately, just one thing is happening. So, of course, in that sense, they are all contained in one another.

Student: I always think of the *I*-consciousness as turning into the wisdom of sameness, so in a sense, the discriminative functioning disappears.

Glassman: I hear you asking, "Doesn't the discriminative functioning vanish when the *I*-consciousness is transmuted into wisdom, the wisdom of equality?" This is the process described in the Zen saying: "First there is a mountain, then there is no mountain, and then there is a mountain." At the point where there is no mountain, the discriminative mind is eclipsed or suspended because you and the mountain have become one; there is no separateness. As you move beyond that, once again there is a mountain, there is a return of the discriminative function, but on a very different level and coming from a different place.

This *I*-consciousness becomes the wisdom of equality, which leads directly to the wisdom of subtle observation, which is seeing the differences. First, seeing the oneness, then seeing the differences from the standpoint of oneness; we can't stay stuck in the realm of the wisdom of equality. Mirror-like wisdom is nothing but seeing that oneness and differences are two sides of the same thing. Then drop all traces of any kind of wisdom, and we're just functioning the way we're supposed to. But it's quite different now; it's pure wisdom.

When we start grabbing hold of one aspect or one stage of this process and say, "Now I am at this stage," then saying so itself causes the wisdom to return to ignorance. So, we get stuck.

Student: A person comes along and asks me my name, and I say, "I'm Bob." Then you say, "I'm Tetsugen," and I say, "I'm Tetsugen, too." That's being one with everything to the point where I'm everybody. I'm Tetsugen, I'm Roshi, I'm Helen, or Helen's me; it's all one state.

Glassman: That's all right, but you musn't get stuck there. It's also true that I'm Tetsugen and that's Helen and that's Bob. You must see that oneness and difference are both true at the same time, and then forget about all of that.

Student: Are they both true at the same instant?

Glassman: Sure.

Student: Or are you shifting from one to the other?

Glassman: No, no shifting. In that respect, there is also no such thing as separate instants. My hands are me, right? My hands are also my hands. Both are true at the same time. It's not that at one instant my hands are me, and at another instant they are my hands. In the saying, "first a mountain is a mountain, then it's no longer a mountain, then it's a mountain again," what's the difference between the first and the third sentence?

Student: Supposedly we go through some authentic change and look at the mountain in a different way.

Glassman: What's this authentic change? Does the mountain change from green to purple?

Student: No, my attitude changes and comes from a different place.

Glassman: How does your attitude change? It's a key point. Having gone through this phase of the wisdom of equality, we've changed the base on which we're standing. Before having kensho, before seeing the oneness of things, certainly we see all the differences: this is me, that's everybody else, all the different things are present. Then we experience oneness, we realize what buddha nature is. This then becomes the basis for everything. Seeing the differences, then, becomes what we call subtle observation, instead of just ordinary observation. When we express it in words, it sounds the same. We still say, "I'm here and you're there," but there has been a big qualitative change. To make that subtle change, we have to experience the wisdom of equality. What we mean when we say "kensho" is not to discover a buddha, not to get something that we don't already have, but just to see the buddha that's been there all along.

Maezumi Roshi spoke about four wisdoms: wisdom of equality, wisdom of subtle observation, mirror-like wisdom, and pure wisdom. First, the kensho experience transforms the *I*-consciousness into the wisdom of equality. Then the wisdom of subtle observation corresponds to our conscious awareness, followed by mirror-like wisdom corresponding to the alaya or storehouse consciousness. Finally, pure wisdom corresponds to the senses. Maezumi Roshi has translated it as "pure," but the sense of it is "functioning wisdom." It's more like the very fact that the eyes see, and the ears hear. I think the reason he used "pure" originally was because there is nothing extra added; just the very functioning of our senses. When you walk, you walk. It doesn't have any of the smell of this wisdom of equality. When we talk about these wisdoms, they seem like special phases that we go through, but then finally it's all quite natural.

15: "Avoiding Idle Talk"

Dogen Zenji's Text

Eighth: *Avoiding idle talk:*
Having realization and being free from discrimination is what is called "avoiding idle talk." To totally know the true form of all things is the same as being without idle talk.

The Buddha says: "When you monks engage in various kinds of idle talk, your minds are disturbed. Although you have left home and become monks, you are still not liberated. Therefore, you must quickly abandon mind-disturbing idle talk. If you would like to attain the joy of the extinction of delusion, you must first simply extinguish the affliction of idle talk. This is what 'avoiding idle talk' means."

The Buddha says: "You monks should continually and single-mindedly strive to accomplish the Way. Every dharma in the world, whether active or non-active, is characterized by destructibility and unrest. Now please keep quiet and say no more. Time passes on, and I shall enter complete nirvana. This is my final admonition."

Maezumi Roshi's Commentary

IN JAPANESE, the title reads *fukeron*. *Fu* is "negation," *ke* means "to play with," *ron* is "talk or argument," or, in broader terms, any writings, principles, or discourses. We should remember that this teaching is the very last teaching of the Buddha. After expounding all sorts of complicated principles, he finally speaks in these plain words. Therefore, we should carefully consider what the Buddha truly means, and what each of us understands by "idle talk."

As the definition of "avoiding idle talk," the text says, "Having realization and being free from discrimination is what is called 'avoiding idle talk.'" The term *sho*, which I translated as "realization," means also "to confirm" or "to verify," to verify by our whole being what life truly is. By being so, we can be free from discrimination. Otherwise, as long as we talk about things as if they were outside of ourselves, our talk will be idle. In a sense, this is why Buddha mentions "avoiding idle talk" last. It is the result, the fruit of our wisdom. Only after we have overcome the fundamental delusion of a gap between ourselves and others can we really avoid idle talk.

This reminds me of the famous story about Yantou (J. Ganto) and Xuefeng (J. Seppo) in which Xuefeng attains enlightenment on Mount Ao. These two men were close Dharma brothers under Master Deshan (J. Tokusan). One day they were caught in a snowstorm while crossing a mountain pass and had to wait in an old cabin for the snow to stop. Xuefeng spent the time sitting in zazen, while Yantou, who had already attained great enlightenment, napped and took it easy and teased his elder brother for his serious practice. Xuefeng could only reply that somehow his mind was not yet at ease, that he was not quite confident of his own understanding.

Yantou then asked Xuefeng to recount the important enlightenment experiences he had had in twenty or so years of practice, offering to check them for him and to approve or disapprove them. After listening to Xuefeng tell of his three "breakthroughs," Yantou finally commented, "Whatever comes in through the six senses is not the real treasure. It should come up from inside yourself and cover heaven and earth." Hearing this, Xuefeng at last attained great enlightenment, and, dancing around the hut, cried out repeatedly, "Today Xuefeng has attained enlightenment on Mount Ao!"

Everything that comes from outside of us, from someone or someplace else, through reading, through hearing or through seeing, will be a kind of idle talk unless we really understand the very nature of our own being, of our life. Understanding our life, we will then understand everything else as buddha nature itself.

Of course, in the strictest sense, everything we say is idle talk. Before enlightenment or after enlightenment, to the extent that life is life, we have to speak dualistically. Remember the famous words of Qingyuan Weihsin (J. Seigen Isshin): "For thirty years before I had penetrated Zen, when I saw mountains, they were mountains; when I saw rivers, they were rivers. Later, after I had intimately met my master and gained the entry point, when I saw mountains, they were not mountains; when I saw rivers, they were not rivers. But now that I have attained the state of essential repose, when I see mountains, they are just mountains; when I see rivers, they are just rivers." What we say and what realized people say is in a way the same, and yet there is a difference. By confirming it for ourselves, our talk will not be idle.

"To know true form exhaustively is to be without idle talk." The English words "to know" seem too weak; there are all kinds of knowing. In the original version, Dogen Zenji used the word *gujin,* a word which he used quite often. *Gu* means "clarify completely." *Jin* means "exhaustively or thoroughly." "True form" is another key Buddhist term which has the sense of "true reality" or "true wisdom." What is the true face of life? By being discursive, we can't fully realize it. We must thoroughly clarify it in actual practice.

We can also approach this awareness in both a positive way and a negative way. In the negative approach, we can try not to spend time on idle talk. Being aware of what we say, we can avoid unnecessary talk, or talk that creates a sense of separation from others. In the positive approach, we can talk in a way which is not idle. This approach relates again to eliminating the fundamental dichotomy of subject and object. It is interesting that Buddha himself intentionally avoided talking about certain subjects. For example, he did not talk about philosophical subjects such as whether the universe is or is not eternal, or whether a buddha exists or doesn't exist after death. These subjects came to be called in Sanskrit *avyakrta,* "undetermined," or in Japanese, *muki,* matters there is no use arguing over. In this regard, Buddha was fond of telling the story of the man who was shot with a poison arrow. Wouldn't he be wasting his time to ask where the man who shot the arrow came from, or what kind of bow he used? The first concern should be pulling out the arrow. In the same way, Buddha only concerned himself with matters that benefited other beings and helped them toward realization.

Verbal expression is perhaps the most effective, important form of communication and involves more than the voice. Writings can be idle talk. Our own thinking can be idle talk. Even our zazen is filled with idle talk, isn't this right? Regarding speech, it is important to consider the way we talk, what we talk about, even the quality of our voice itself.

Of the Ten Grave Bodhisattva Precepts, or aspects of our practice, four of these concern speech: do not tell a lie; do not be ignorant; do not discuss others' faults and errors; and do not elevate yourself and blame others. That is how important right speech is in our life. Above all, the point is to realize the wholeness of this non-dualistic, non-discriminative life. When we do this thoroughly, this is called enlightenment.

Buddha says, *"Although you have left home and become monks, you are still not liberated,"* simply because you are bound by discrimination and are not free from dichotomy. *"Therefore, you must quickly abandon mind-disturbing idle talk. If you would like to attain the joy of the extinction of delusion, you must first simply extinguish the affliction of idle talk."* This is what we are trying to do when we do shikantaza or work on the koan Mu. We are trying to realize the extinction of delusion. This is being without idle talk.

It is wonderful to see people practicing and growing together. Please thoroughly accomplish your practice. By doing so, you will benefit not only yourself and the people around you, but also many other people. In connection with this eighth awareness, let us be mindful of our speech. Living together, let us not say anything which might harm or hurt other people, or destroy our practice. Let us be kind and helpful as we pursue our practice together.

Discussion

Glassman: We talk about two kinds of expressions in Zen: dead and alive. Using dead words, we express our understanding in such a way that the listener holds onto what we say as an idea or a concept. In this way, we hinder their realization. This is the problem with the Dharma talks we give, and why Zen masters are so reluctant to talk too much. Most of the time, our expressions provide new ideas for attachment.

An alive expression is one in which we don't give people anything to hold on to, but rather something which forces them to reevaluate what they've been doing, or to see it in a different light. An alive expression can be verbal or nonverbal. Somebody coming along and hitting you with the waking stick *(kyosaku)* can be a very alive expression which frees you from where you're stuck. For example, the stick may shift you out of your complacent sitting. This can also be done verbally.

Another way to judge whether your talk is idle or not is by whether it is fostering or disturbing the harmony. Sangha, which is often translated as "harmony," can be looked at in several ways. If we look at the Sangha as the people studying here, then harmony is the relations between the people studying and working together, and idle talk would be talk that interferes with or disrupts the harmony. We can also look at the Sangha as being the relationship between phenomena. When we see the Dharma as all the phenomena that is happening and Buddha as the Supreme Way, or the oneness of everything, the harmony is the inter-relatedness of all phenomena—the fact that oneness is manifesting in many different ways. To see this harmony is mirror-like wisdom. Giving people ideas to cling to disturbs this harmony and hinders another's seeing the way oneness and manyness flow together.

Student: But how can you really interfere with this harmony?

Glassman: These precepts—elevating ourselves by criticizing others, or talking about others' faults—are good examples of how we disturb this harmony. For example, somebody will be upset with what is going on and will go around complaining, rather than doing something about it. This upsets the harmony of the Sangha.

Student: But in some sense, even that doesn't feel like interference.

Glassman: It may or may not be. In a sense, you could say that nothing can upset the harmony, everything is in balance, even when it's out of balance. But in another sense, you can say that idle talk is upsetting to a Sangha.

We always have to look at it from both sides. From the intrinsic standpoint, we're all Buddha, and the Dharma is everything, no matter what we do. The Sangha, the harmony, is simply the relationships between things as they are. From the experiential perspective, we have to practice, and there are things that we can do. We can take these precepts to heart.

What it boils down to is that I'm everything, so if something goes wrong, I have to look at where it has gone wrong in me, and what I am going to do about it. As soon as I start blaming others for it, something is wrong. No matter how much it seems to be another's fault, that's not the place to look. If we truly see that we are everything, then these precepts become expressions of just what is. As long as we don't see this, then we blame others, disrupt the harmony, which hurts the Sangha.

Student: Extending what we're saying right now about the harmony and Sangha relations, can you give me an example that shows "avoiding idle talk?"

Glassman: Eliminate the self.

Student: Do you also include as talk musicians playing music and artists drawing or sculpting?

Glassman: Instead of using the word *talk,* use *expression;* "avoid idle expressions" encompasses a great deal. The Buddha is also including thinking itself. Buddha says, *"Having realization and being free from discrimination."* That would involve every function, not necessarily just talking or other external forms of expression.

Again, we can consider two perspectives: the specific and the general. In a specific sense, almost everything we do is idle talk or discrimination. In a general sense, then you could say that nothing we do is idle talk. Everything is just an expression of our buddha nature; everything is perfect as it is. From this perspective, talking about something is fine.

To find a middle ground between these two perspectives, a sense of appropriateness is really helpful. There are times when talking about practice is actually idle talk, such as when you're all wound up in yourself. It's easier to tune into a situation and be appropriate when you are not self-absorbed.

Student: How about just plain, wasting-time talking?

Glassman: This may be why the Buddha described this activity as idle talk. Often, if we're discriminating between ourselves and others, we use talk as a way of cushioning. I like the word *appropriateness.* And I also love to talk.

Student: In Chögyam Trungpa Rinpoche's book *Cutting Through Spiritual Materialism,* there is a chapter on the bodhisattva vow that says that compassion and communication are one and the same thing.

Glassman: I think so. If you're really compassionate, there's no way you could not reach out to others. Communication can take many forms, but being compassionate certainly means having to communicate. Somehow, people come to the conclusion that the best thing to do is not to talk at all; whatever you say seems wrong, so why say anything at all? We must communicate, but everybody's idea about how to do this is different.

Trungpa Rinpoche has another phrase I like, "idiot compassion." There are people running around being nice mostly for their own sake. It is very important to cultivate the wisdom of knowing how to be compassionate, and then to practice being more skillful at it. We say that compassion is the function of prajna wisdom; that is, wisdom and compassion are the same thing. When our expressions are truly the functioning of wisdom, then we are avoiding idle talk.

IV: AN EXPERIENCE
OF ENLIGHTENMENT

Editors' Preface to Part IV

THE PERSONAL MEMOIR which follows was written by Flora Eko Courtois in response to a request from Hakuun Yasutani Roshi. It was initially published in a small private edition by the Zen Center of Los Angeles in the early 1970s. A decade later, it was reissued in a somewhat larger edition by the Theosophical Publishing House.

Since its original publication, the culture of American Buddhism has exploded, and a new generation of practitioners is now flourishing—but when it was written, there were few such first-person accounts apart from the handful in Roshi Philip Kapleau's landmark volume, *The Three Pillars of Zen*. Even today, it is rare to have such an intimate and detailed account of not only a deep enlightenment experience, but also of its subsequent maturation and integration.

As with all first-person accounts of enlightenment, readers are encouraged to read with caution, lest these accounts become a concretized set of ideas about how experiences of awakening "should" look or feel. Especially if one is not practicing in regular personal contact with a qualified Zen teacher, such ideas can easily become an impediment in one's practice. While Flora's account is similar in general terms to classical descriptions of enlightenment experiences, the reader must bear in mind that each awakening is unique to the person, place, and time in which it occurs.

The period of the 1940s in which these experiences unfolded were marked by an absence of an American Buddhist practice culture. There was also a lack of qualified teachers to help guide the practitioner to contextualize these experiences both before and after awakening and to navigate through the process of maturation and integration which are so crucial in Zen practice. To the casual observer, Flora's account of her moods and behaviors might even appear to be manic—but it would be a serious error to so pathologize her in this way.

The experience of awakening, especially when profound, can evoke a very natural release of ecstatic energy and great joy, a joy so intense as to overflow the conventional bounds of restraint. Unlike mania, however, this celebratory enthusiasm normally subsides as the individual gradually integrates her experiences and settles into a quieter, less openly extraordinary state. Such was clearly the case with Flora Eko Courtois.

Not long before her death, Flora asked that her account be republished. Although she had planned some revision, she unfortunately died before it could be completed. This volume, then, is in fulfillment of a promise made while she was still living. It is particularly fitting that it appear in this edition of *The Hazy Moon of Enlightenment,* as her study and practice with both Yasutani Roshi and Maezumi Roshi was so significant a part of the last decades of her life.

We hope that her story will serve to inspire others, as it has us, to follow the path of awakening, and to penetrate the Great Matter of life and death together.

In youthful days
You had doubt about this life
No teacher found
And went alone
At the moment of glancing at the desk
The doubt disappeared, the mind in peace
You lost your way and now
The way has opened in all directions

Written for Flora Courtois
by Hakuun Yasutani Roshi

16: An Experience of Enlightenment

Flora Courtois

SEARCH

WHEN AND WHERE does this story begin? It is difficult to say. Even now I remember the feeling as a small child that all things about me, the people, the animals, trees and flowers, my dolls, my plate and spoon, all participated with me in one vivid reality. It was a family joke that I had to be spoken to several times to get my attention, so absorbed did I often become in listening and watching, in playing with my dolls and, later on, in reading. Often I felt in magic communion with other living things. Some of my earliest memories are of rescuing drowning insects from a small pond, of escorting small spiders from the house so they would not be killed, of lying on my stomach in a neighboring field, raptly absorbed in the busy life of the tiny creatures under the giant grass blades.

Despite these empathic experiences of early childhood, by the time I was thirteen or fourteen years old I had become a self-centered, self-conscious girl. It was as if I'd lost track of who I was. I daydreamed a good deal about being popular among many friends; in actuality I was nervous and isolated, not knowing how to be comfortable with young people my age and anxiously searching for some role to play in life. At times, what I felt to be my inner voice seemed to be trying to draw me away from the busy life and activities of my friends. It was as if I were of two minds and this sometimes left me confused and unable to act at all. Probably these were normal adolescent feelings intensified by the pressures of being ahead of my age and usual grade in school.

When I was sixteen, minor surgery had to be performed. An ether cone was placed over my face and as I breathed in deeply, a great whirling spiral of light approached from an enormous distance and at great speed. At the same time, a voice of unmistakable authority seemed to say that when the center of the spiral reached me I would "understand all things." Just as the center reached me I blacked out, but after recovering there remained an unforgettable conviction that what I had heard and seen was in some inexplicable way the deepest truth.

Sometime during my seventeenth year, quietly, unobtrusively, a process began which was to build up over a period of several years until it literally took over my life. This began with a growing sense of doubt which spread until it encompassed everything I'd been taught and everything I knew. In the house where we were living there was a number of books of maxims written by the great persons of many ages. I read these, collecting favorite sayings in a scrapbook which I still have. However, I began to think it strange that with all the books of advice in the world, all the laws and admonitions from parents, teachers, priests, and other elders, there was still nothing to assure me of living fully in any given moment, since every moment was unique. How did one fit the rule to reality when by the time one found the right rule the moment was gone?

In a vague, groping way I now began to search for some single law, some one basic Reality so primary that it permeated all else. I had been brought up as a Catholic. Each Sunday I dutifully attended Mass with neither much understanding nor any real sense of participation. I was an onlooker and I felt ashamed of this. The problem, I concluded, must lie in the fact that I didn't understand my religion. So shortly thereafter I made my way to the study of the parish priest, where, sitting on the edge of my chair, I asked him to explain these matters to me. He went over the various doctrines of the church, of the Trinity and the Virgin Birth, of salvation and redemption, to make sure I knew them. I felt intensely disappointed that he didn't seem to come to the core of the matter. He then sent me home with three or four books to read further on doctrine. Dutifully I read them all only to finish with more questions and doubts than ever. I clearly remember thinking: "Surely there must be *something* that applies even to the everyday tasks of life, even to how I wash the dishes at night. But how do I *find* it?"

If not in church, I decided, then certainly back in school, in the works of the great philosophers, the answers would come. At this time I had finished one year of college and then had to stay at home a year because of the economic depression. Now through a tremendous effort I returned to the University of Michigan in Ann Arbor, borrowing the tuition, arranging to help with the housework and care of children in a home about three miles from the campus in return for my room and board, and at the same time taking a nearly full class load. This busy schedule of homework and classwork was all on the surface, however, because underneath—walking back and forth to campus, doing my chores—I became increasingly preoccupied with pursuing my doubts to their limits. During the following year or more, with a desperate intensity, I read from the works of most of the leading Western philosophers from Plato to Spinoza, Hume, Berkeley, and on to Kant, Hegel, Schopenhauer, Nietzsche, Bradley, Kierkegaard, Bergson, Wittgenstein, and others. Fascinating as much of it was, it all seemed fragmented and one-sided. Nothing satisfied me, nothing went to the root of my need. I seemed to be moving in endless theoretical and verbal circles, chasing a mirage of ultimate finality. At times I had periods of bleak despair, feeling my quest was hopeless.

Then one day, in a psychology class, the instructor made a casual remark to the effect that the world as we saw it was "simply a projection of neural activity in the visual centers of the brain." I walked out of the class and along the street, thunderstruck, saying over and over to myself, "All I know, the whole world, even the universe, is myself! The answer somehow lies in myself." I was filled with an extraordinary sense of exhilaration with this realization.

Shortly after this, another incident occurred which made a deep impression on me. Standing at the kitchen window one day, and looking out at where a path wound under some maple trees, I suddenly saw the scene with a freshness and clarity that I'd never seen before. Simultaneously, as though for the first time, I fully realized I was not only on the earth but of it, an intimate part and product of it. A door had briefly opened. I stood there transfixed. I remember thinking: "Distant places on the map such as Tibet and North Africa are extensions of right here, all interrelated!" For a long time I had been reading books on how to swim; now, for a moment, I had plunged into real water.

After these two incidents, I ceased to search for an answer in reading and became intensely interested in exploring everyday experience. The very nature of sensation itself absorbed my attention. I became increasingly aware of sights, sounds, touch, smells, and feelings, all for their own sakes, and the more observant I became, the more endless the vistas which seemed to open. "What is more immediate than sensation?" I asked myself. "Surely Reality must somehow permeate immediate sensation. Yet each sense is so limited, so partial and incomplete. How does one sense Reality whole, all at once? Is that impossible?"

Like a strong undertow pulling me down and away from the routine surface of life, my inner quest absorbed more and more of my time. I began to stay alone in my room for long periods, just sitting, observing, struggling inwardly for some direct contact. "If there is a basic Reality that is common to everything," I thought, "it must be *within* my experience too, as well as in everything and everybody else's. Surely I can grasp it immediately and at first hand. Any other way would be only second hand and would not be *it* at all. But how could I get at it, how could I know it first hand?" I became preoccupied with the most elementary processes of getting myself reoriented to the earth and to the people and things around me. It's difficult to describe this period and the rather eerie feelings that pervaded this groping. It was as if I had been living in a world of ideas; now, having lost confidence in these and having let go of them, I had to start all over again—looking at everything, feeling, touching, and sensing it again almost as an infant does—to realize what experience truly was.

Again and again I returned to considering the sense of sight. It seemed to me that *how* one saw the world around one, not *what* one saw but *how*, was the crux of the problem. Somewhere in a psychology textbook, perhaps in a chapter on gestalt psychology, I had read a discussion of figure and ground perception. I now noticed that while the focus of sight moved from figure to figure, the nature of the ground largely determined the nature of the figure. But what and where was the basic ground for all perception? Was it just another, but larger, figure with a fixed boundary? I seemed unable either to penetrate to its nature or to find its limits.

It came to me that I had always thought of the center of myself as in my head and the rest of my body as somehow incidental. My head was so full of activity it was almost as if it were disconnected from the rest of me. Just before falling asleep sometimes I would have the illusion of having an enormous head. I thought of the various parts of my body in sequence. It seemed to me there was something wrong with all this. If one were a whole and single human being, surely there must be some way to realize oneself all at once, to think with one's feet as well as with one's head.

My pursuit of this elusive ground of all things perceived began now to bring to my attention a welter of forgotten memories and feelings. Over many hours I reviewed past experiences with parents, relatives, and friends, realizing gradually that this web of memories made an ever-shifting pattern, never quite the same from moment to moment. Where was the changelessness in change I sought here?

Now it was as if I were being pulled down into the vortex of a maelstrom within me, pulling me ever further down and away from everyday life and involving me in an all-consuming life or death struggle. Although I never completely lost touch with other people around me, I began to wonder if I would ever be in close communication with other human beings again. Their lives and daily preoccupations seemed so remote from mine. The simplest tasks distracted me and took an excessive amount of time. I remember standing over an ironing board and concentrating so intently on the question: What is the ground of everyday reality? that it took me all afternoon to do a small ironing. This was certainly no way to hold a job!

I remembered a remark of Nietzsche's that it was dangerous for anyone to go too far alone. This frightened me but I could not give up now. I felt compelled to go on no matter what the outcome.

Now I made two urgent attempts to find someone who could understand and help. One Sunday morning I went back to Mass, which I had no longer been attending, at the campus chapel.

It was a clear, cold day and the chapel was jammed with other young people dressed in their best clothes. The priest was a popular, hearty young man who kept the social life of the parish churning. The whole ritual affair appeared to me, in my frame of mind, as a highly mannered charade. After listening to his sermon, the possibility of ever communicating my acute concern to this man seemed remote. Perhaps I did him an injustice but I never went back.

I next paid a visit to a philosophy professor whom I'd heard was a kind and understanding man. When I told him of my intense interest in discovering the nature of Reality, he suggested I take a course in epistemology the following term. I left his office feeling utterly forsaken, thinking, "I don't want another course. What I want is *the thing itself!*" I began to despair of ever communicating this to anyone.

About this time, when in my room alone, I began to have occasional visions. These were not hallucinations nor were they dreams. They were more like the visions one sometimes sees just before sleep. They were astoundingly clear. In one of them, a scene appeared as from an incalculably remote and primitive time. I seemed to be a member of a small family of cave dwellers. There was a darkness, a gloomy dankness about our lives and surroundings. In our cave we had found a place of security and protection from what I sensed to be a hostile world. Gradually, however, we found within ourselves the courage as a family to venture forth together to seek a brighter, more open place. Now we found ourselves on a great, open plain which stretched in all directions and where the horizons seemed to beckon to us with untold possibilities. To my surprise and horror, the others in my family found this threatening and decided to retreat to life in the cave again. I felt profoundly convinced that this represented a critical decision, a fork in the life of the family and indeed of the whole human race. The challenge was of the next important step upward. I now knew that the choice I had to make was whether to remain within the safe fold of the group or to continue on, leaving most of humanity behind. If I went on, henceforth I would go alone.

After this, my sense of aloneness deepened still further. In another vision, I found myself standing in a familiar room where apparently I had already spent many years. The place had an abstract, geometric quality, squared off in flat, two-dimensional planes as in certain modern stage sets. I seemed to spend a great deal of my time at a desk facing a wall, manipulating assorted colored blocks. Without actually seeing them, I also knew that all around me in the same building, up and down long hallways, there were others in similar cubistic rooms, busy day and night with the same kind of abstract manipulations. Once in a while we came out of our rooms and met in the hallways to chat awhile before returning to our separate cubicles. One day, without knowing why or how, I turned completely around and there to my surprise was a long, open window opening directly on to a breathtaking vista. It had apparently been there all along.

Stepping outside in wonder, I found myself again in an airy, light scene where there was a mountain-fresh stream winding beneath shade trees, where the colors were deep and translucent; everything seemed alive and dancing and the horizons and the firmament extended to infinity in all directions. Along with everything else, I seemed to dance in ecstasy. Then, standing still and looking back at the building, I thought sadly of the people in their cubicles, unaware of the wondrous universe all about, so easily accessible if only they would turn around and look. I felt I must return to communicate this message to them.

To my dismay, on reentering the building I found I had no words for it. Nothing I did could alert the attention of these others running up and down the halls or working furiously in their walled-off rooms.

It is hard to adequately describe the depth of conviction, the sense of mysterious truth these visions carried with them. A conviction grew in me that humanity had become over-civilized and degenerate. Just as in my visions, somewhere on the evolutionary path, a wrong fork had been taken where people had retreated from a critical challenge to return to the living source, walling themselves off and manipulating their constricted environments. They had become effete, intellectual creatures out of communion with the rest of nature. I began to seriously consider the possibility that I might have to go into the woods to live a more wholesome life alone with the animals (at the same time hoping that a few human beings with similar feelings might eventually join me there!).

I now developed messianic feelings about having to write down these "truths." I began to write a long paper, sitting up far into the night for several nights. The general theme of the paper was that the human race was lost and could save itself only by returning to its roots in nature. When it was finished, I telephoned Dr. DeWitt Parker, my philosophy professor, and persuaded him to let me bring the paper to his house that very evening. It was a bitter winter night with waist deep snow, so in my urgency I called a taxi, a wild extravagance for me then. I had a swollen lip from a bad cold sore and I must have been a strange, disheveled, half-mad sight as I stood on Dr. Parker's doorstep, manuscript clutched in my hand. Sitting at one end of his pleasant living room, Dr. Parker patiently read through the entire paper while I sat nearby anxiously waiting. When he had finished, he told me in a kindly manner that the paper made him think of Rousseau. Then, as he was showing me to the door, he gently suggested that it might be wise for me to have a little talk with the University psychiatrist. As I returned to my room that night, I felt my last hope of ever being understood had vanished.

Two days later, as I passed a corner drug store, I went in and bought a large bottle of sleeping pills (for which no prescription was apparently then required in Michigan) thinking that, if my isolation from the rest of humanity became any deeper, I might take them. That evening, looking at my face in the bathroom mirror, I looked quite unreal to myself. Yet what I was discovering seemed more real than the everyday life around me. How strange it all was.

Fortunately, two incidents soon occurred. My seat in a class in European history was in the front row center directly in front of the lecturer, so that as he leaned over his lectern he looked directly down at me. The lecturer happened to be a young, visiting professor from Oxford, very British, very starchy. Sitting in my seat in class one midwinter morning, gazing straight ahead, I suddenly became aware of space in an extraordinary manner; that is, I was equally aware of it behind me, underneath, above, all around and, in fact, it seemed to be all through me. This so astounded me that I held my eyes wide open and my breath still for fear of losing this incredible experience. This was too much for the visiting Britisher who brought his lecture to a full stop, leaned over the lectern, and asked me if something he had said had unduly surprised me. I blinked, breathed, replied, "No, sir," and returned to history. But now I knew something extraordinary was very close, and I felt exhilarated and hopeful.

Apparently by now, a number of people were becoming concerned about my unusual behavior and someone had made a telephone call.

One evening there was a knock on my bedroom door and Dr. Bell, a woman doctor from the University student health service, paid me a visit. After a short talk she persuaded me that a few days' rest in the infirmary would be a sound idea, so I packed a few things and went with her. Next morning found me in the office of the University psychiatrist, Dr. Theophile Rafael. Dr. Rafael asked me a number of questions about my life at home and in school, and I talked to him quite freely about my parents and my school life. We never once discussed my deeper and more urgent concerns, but I did tell him of my vision of the open window. He had a most understanding manner of nodding his head to one side, his forefinger resting alongside his nose. I realize now he probably interpreted this account of mine from a Freudian point of view. At the time, all I felt was a profound relief at being back in contact with at least one seemingly understanding member of the human race. I saw Dr. Rafael only once or twice more in his office. He and his assistant decided I had been working too hard and eating too little. These kind people managed to tap a University fund which enabled me to move to a rooming house nearer campus, and for a few, wonderfully free months, I simply went to one of the college cafeterias where all my meals were paid for. They also requested that I drop in at intervals and report how things were going. This I gladly did.

It was now early spring. After my stay of four or five days in the infirmary, I moved into my new room and returned to my underground quest with renewed vigor. Sitting on a bus one day, I concentrated intently on trying to recapture the awareness of open, empty space in all directions, until I suddenly realized several people sitting opposite were staring at me in some alarm.

I finally decided that Reality must be unlike any preconceived idea I might have of it and reached a point of just waiting and letting be. For long periods I simply sat, saying inwardly "No, not this" as if waiting, for what I knew not.

Sometime in April, Easter vacation arrived, and I went home to Detroit to spend a week with my parents. There, about three days later, alone in my room, sitting quietly on the edge of my bed and gazing at a small desk, not thinking of anything at all, in a moment too short to measure, the universe turned on its axis and my search was over.

ARRIVAL

The small, pale green desk at which I'd been so thoughtlessly gazing had totally and radically changed. It appeared now with a clarity, a depth of three-dimensionality, a freshness I had never imagined possible. At the same time, in a way that is utterly indescribable, all my questions and doubts were gone as effortlessly as chaff in the wind. I knew everything and all at once, yet not in the sense that I had ever known anything before.

All things were the same in my little bedroom yet totally changed. Still sitting in wonder on the edge of my narrow bed, one of the first things I realized was that the focus of my sight seemed to have changed; it had sharpened to an infinitely small point, which moved ceaselessly in paths totally free of the old accustomed ones, as if flowing from a new source.

What on earth had happened? So released from all tension, so ecstatically light did I feel, I seemed to float down the hall to the bathroom to look at my face in the mottled mirror over the sink. The pupils of my eyes were dark, dilated and brimming with mirth. With wondrous relief, I began to laugh from the soles of my feet upward.

Within a few days I had returned to Ann Arbor, and over a period of many months a ripening took place, a deepening and unfolding of this experience, which filled me with wonder and gratitude at every moment. The foundations of my world had fallen. I had plunged into a numinous openness which had obliterated all fixed distinctions including that of *within* and *without*. A Presence had absorbed the universe including myself, and to this I surrendered in absolute confidence. Often, without any particular direction in mind, I found myself outside running along the street in joyous abandon. Sometimes when alone, I simply danced as freely as I did as a child. The whole world seemed to have reversed itself, to have turned outside in. Activity flowed simply and effortlessly, and to my amazement, seemingly without thought. Instead of following my old sequence of learning, thinking, planning, then acting, action had taken precedence and whatever was learned was surprisingly incidental. Yet nothing ever seemed to go out of bounds; there was no alternation between self-control and letting go, but rather a perfect rightness and spontaneity to all this flowing activity.

This new kind of knowing was so pure and unadorned, so delicate, that nothing in the language of my past could express it. Neither sense nor feeling nor imagination contained it, yet all were contained in it. In some indefinable way, I knew with absolute certainty the universe with its changeless unity and harmony in change, and the inseparability of all seeming opposites.

It was as if, before all this occurred, "I" had been a fixed point inside my head looking out at a world out there, a separate and comparatively flat world. The periphery of awareness had now come to light, yet neither fixed periphery nor center existed as such. A paradoxical quality seemed to permeate all existence. Feeling myself centered as never before, at the same time I knew the whole universe to be centered at every point. Having plunged to the center of emptiness, having lost all purposefulness in the old sense, I had never felt so one-pointed, so clear and decisive. Freed from separateness, feeling one with the universe, everything including myself had become at once unique and equal. If God was the word for this Presence in which I was absorbed, then everything was either holy or nothing; no distinction was possible. All was meaningful, complete as it was, each bird, bud, midge, mole, atom, crystal, of total importance in itself. As in the notes of a great symphony, nothing was large or small, nothing of more or less importance to the whole. I now saw that wholeness and holiness are one.

Passing the campus chapel, I remembered how I had been taught in church to think of myself as here on earth and of God as above and out there, to aspire to heaven as in some future time and place, to emulate the lives of others. How tragic it seemed that anyone should be distracted in this way from a first-hand knowledge of Reality. My entire education had taught me only to stand in the light. Nothing had been added, but only the delusions of this education removed. I knew now that eternity is here always, that there is no higher, no deeper, no separate past or future time or place. How could love be other than this all-encompassing Oneness to which we can do nothing but open ourselves?

I felt that I was done forever with all seeking, all philosophic and religious doctrines, all fear of dying or concern for the future, all need for authority other than this. If I could continue in this state of "Open Vision," I felt certain that whatever happened, everything would be right just as it was.

Years before I had sought a rule that would apply to everything I did, even to washing dishes. Now I simply washed the dishes. In the most simple of bodily feelings and the most ordinary of daily tasks, living was transformed. I had never felt so completely whole and in one piece, or enjoyed my bodily feelings so much. Breathing had changed, had become deeper, more rhythmical. Hands, eyes, voice, all seemed quieter, more relaxed. With seemingly boundless energy, every task became effortless and light. Running exuberantly home from classes or work, bounding up two flights of stairs to my third-floor room, I would fall soundly asleep for a quick, daytime catnap, then waken shortly feeling wonderfully refreshed. With spontaneous gusto, I found myself eating lightly whenever hungry (gaining ten much-needed pounds in a few months). Even my handwriting changed.

As for my relations with others, another person now filled my shoes. Laughter and delight seemed to fill my life. Somehow I had become more human, more ordinary, more friendly and at ease with all kinds of people. Apparently I appeared happy and smiling too, for strangers often came up and spoke to me.

I had no idea what I could have done to have deserved these miraculous changes, but I felt the most inexpressible gratitude for them. They had enriched my life beyond compare. Literally everything had become interesting. As for my school work, it improved in some areas and declined in others. I was less concerned with meeting conventional demands.

But of all the changes that had occurred, the one that seemed to me in some mysterious way to be the key to everything else was the change in vision. It was as if some inner eye, some ancient center of awareness, which extended equally and at once in all directions without limit and which had been there all along, had been restored. This inner vision seemed to be anchored in infinity in a way that was detached from immediate sight and, yet at the same time, had a profound effect on sight. Walking along the street I was aware of the street flowing past and beneath me, the trees or buildings moving past all around, and the sky moving above as if I were immersed in one flowing whole. A childlike unknowing pervaded perception. The immediate world had acquired a new depth and clarity of color and form, an unalloyed freshness and unexpectedness. Rooted in the present, every moment opened to eternity. Along with this, there was a sharp single-pointedness to the focus of attention which caused me to feel that I was looking straight and deeply into whatever entered my attention. Yet paradoxically I felt blind. This is difficult to describe. It was as if my attention were now rooted in some deeper center so that my everyday sight, my eyes, were released from their former tension and were now free.

Another incidental change I noticed was that no matter in what direction I looked, no shadow of my nose or face ever appeared in the clear field of sight, as apparently it had occasionally done before. I also found other people's eyes fascinating, as well as those of animals, looking into them as if into my own. This change of vision was so impressive that I went to the University Medical School library and searched in the card files under the headings of vision, sight, and eyes, trying to find some reference to this new kind of vision. There was nothing, not a clue. Still I remained convinced that this change in vision was somehow basic to all the other transforming changes.

What I called "Open Vision" not only awakened appreciation for the inexhaustible delights of everyday living—the smell of burning leaves, the taste of fresh Michigan apples, the song of the thrush in the early morning. It had also made me more aware of the sufferings of others, so much of it self-inflicted. Knowing that it was perhaps impossible, I still longed to tell others something that would help open their vision as mine had been. My first attempt was with my friend Suzanne, a piano student. To her I said something like this: "Sue, there is a way to know the universe and yourself as one whole, all at once. If you can do that you won't have to strain so to learn. It will come naturally." We talked frequently until I realized I was not really communicating this to her at all. Another day, near the University health service, I ran into my old friend the psychiatrist, Dr. Rafael. "How are you getting along?" he said. "Sometime if you'd have time," I said, "I'd like to come in and tell you about a wonderful thing that's happened to my vision." He gave me a long, quizzical look. "Well," he said, "I wouldn't worry about my vision if I were you. You're looking awfully well." And off he went.

About this time, a paper was required of me in a general science class. My background in any physical science was almost non-existent at that

time, but I recklessly decided to try to put down on paper, in the objective language of science, what I felt I had discovered through changed
vision. The paper was titled "One Law." It was another unsuccessful
attempt. My professor commented that he had no idea about what I was
talking.

How inadequate words were to even suggest this experience to anyone else. What seemed to me the most marvelous and significant of
experiences seemed hardly of passing interest to others.

I came to feel that to talk about this personal experience was to
expose to shallow interpretation and disrespect what was most worthy
of respect. I decided then never to speak of it again until I was confident
it would be appreciated.

Autumn came to Ann Arbor, bringing with it a carnival of colors and
sparkling air. Wandering in the fields and along wooded paths, sometimes lying on a grassy bank looking up at the stars in the evening, I felt
completely at home. In an indefinable way, I felt the presence of others
who understood, and I felt confident that so long as I lived with Open
Vision, everything else would somehow be right and just as it had
always been intended.

So it came about that the changes described here, so strange and
incredible at first, gradually came to seem quite natural.

Loss and Return

For the next year-and-a-half or two, I lived each day with joyful awareness. It never occurred to me to think of myself as in any way enlightened. I had never heard such terms as *enlightenment,* or *religious
experience,* let alone *kensho.* If I had heard of Buddhism at all, it was
simply as an obscure Asian religion.

By now, I had married and was working in Detroit. During this time,
I read a book entitled *The Bates Method of Sight Without Glasses.* The
author, Dr. Bates, impressed me as having an unusual point of view
about seeing. I was struck by his frequent use of the term "central fixa-
tion" and wondered if by any chance he might understand about Open
Vision. With a little investigation, I discovered that Dr. Bates was
deceased, but that his widow lived and carried on his work in New York

City. I resolved to go there and talk to her. After saving up for many months, I made the trip to New York where I visited Mrs. Bates. She was a kind, friendly person. We had a most pleasant visit, but this experience taught me that she was talking about local sight while I was struggling to express an entirely different dimension of vision.

Back again in Detroit, I was becoming ever more dissatisfied with my job as a professional writer in the business world. Quite naively, I decided that by becoming a psychologist, I might find a way to deepen my own experience and also bring it to others. I had long since concluded that organized religion offered me no help in this way. Once again, I returned to study at the University, now changing my major from English literature to psychology.

Here one day, seemingly by accident, I picked up a copy of William James's *Varieties of Religious Experience* and, with a shock of recognition, read for the first time descriptions of the kind of experience I had had. This led me directly to Asian literature. When I read the *Tao Te Ching* and soon after, my first Buddhist sutra, tears filled my eyes. They struck such a familiar chord. The sutras seemed to speak with unveiled clarity. Mandalas fascinated me. I wondered if anyone living had had such an experience as mine, or if mine were some kind of anomaly.

After we had moved to California, I continued my exploration of oriental literature, reading my first book on Zen, discovering the works of such western mystics as Meister Eckhart, John of the Cross, William Blake, and the author of *The Cloud of Unknowing*. I felt an especial affinity with Eckhart and Blake. The term mystical seemed to me to be a misnomer for these authors, expressing as they did so deep a grasp of Reality.

In about 1950, I took a course in comparative religion from a Buddhist scholar at a nearby university. At this professor's home, I met a writer of popular books on Zen Buddhism. I listened in rapt attention as these learned men talked at great length about Buddhism. Yet no mention of practice of any kind was ever made.

It must have been about this time that I began to feel a subtle pride in knowing first-hand what these authorities apparently knew only in theory. I began to think of myself as someone who had had an experience of enlightenment and was therefore secretly special. Like one with an old sickness that had lain dormant for many years, I developed a new kind of egotism more pernicious than ever before because it was accompanied by a sense of possessing special and superior knowledge.

My college career, which had been interrupted so many times by the need to work, by wartime and the demands of family life, was finally completed at a Southern California college. In a psychology department of good academic standing in those years, for a student to make a serious study of any aspect of religious or mystical experience was not acceptable. The closest I came to doing so was to write several papers referring to the extensive literature on authentic religious experiences from all times and places. Once or twice, I pointed out such accounts in the works of William James to a psychologist or psychiatrist on the teaching staff. The reaction was invariably to label them as "psychotic episodes" or "regression in the service of the ego." Finally, I became interested in a subject which seemed related to the opening of inner vision, that is, to changes in perception during states of deep relaxation, since one of the clearest recollections from my own experience was of the wonderful release of all tension.

At graduation time, the head of the psychology department encouraged me to go on to graduate school at a nearby university to develop this interest in studying for a doctorate. For the next few years, I became immersed in a high-pressure graduate school machine. The compulsion to be scientific seemed to narrow and constrict everyone's perspective, leading us all to an obsessive concern with counting and measuring. No orthodox church was ever more rigidly doctrinaire.

The necessity to regurgitate quantities of busy work to earn good grades made original work virtually impossible. In over twenty graduate courses, I made what seemed to the faculty to be an impressive record of A grades for what seemed to me to be a mediocre quality of performance. Since no one shared my unconventional interest in the effect of deep relaxation on perception, the only way to pursue this interest was on my own. This I did, also studying during these years physics, biology, mathematics, and western philosophy, as well as working actively as a psychologist in several clinics. As an adjunct to my training, I underwent an orthodox psychoanalysis.

The clinical psychology students were essentially oriented toward escaping from graduate school at the earliest moment, with a union-card diploma and a portfolio of formulas to apply to future patients. However exhaustively we tested those unfortunate and troubled patients on whom we practiced at the University clinic, somehow they belonged in none of our categories. How often I wondered if the more psychotic of these patients might only have lost their way in searching for a deeper, truer perception of Reality than that perceived by a possibly miseducated therapist.

I became increasingly of two minds about all this: on the one hand, stimulated by the university atmosphere, on the other, disturbed by a sense of wandering further and further off course. To the extent that I had become academically successful, I had become in a deeper sense unwise, unintelligent, unfree, and unloving.

This busy life was suddenly interrupted by the necessity for some major surgery and a prolonged convalescence. Lying quietly alone, I realized I had lost my way in the midst of all this diversity. All the knowledge I had accumulated in these years could not be compared to that which I had learned in one measureless moment long before. Every formal subject led to the same abyss.

So a decision was made, and against the advice of every interested faculty member, I terminated my studies for a lesser degree, a masters, and returned to a quieter and more ordinary life. Now I spent more time with my family, read and wrote poetry, helped my husband when needed with business, and worked occasionally as a volunteer in the community.

But in those intellectually busy years, I had built no inner bulwark against a deep despair I often began to feel in the early '60s. I grieved that the priceless opportunity I had been given in my youth somehow had been dissipated and wasted. All my efforts to communicate what seemed most important to me had failed. Never once had I found the way to pass it on directly to anyone else, not even to my family. There seemed to be no one to whom I could even speak of this. I longed for guidance both religious and practical. I also longed to be a member of a truly religious community. When, for one reason or another, I attended one of our community's churches, all I seemed to find was an organized effort to protect and distract people from the awesome struggle and dangers of transformation.

Over a period of several years, during many long nights, I lived with that profound sense of abandonment called by St. John of the Cross the "dark night of the soul." On the surface my life looked successful enough. But on the deepest level, I felt I had failed in living every day in joyful awareness, a source of tender patience and calm strength to my family and others.

My only hope lay in my confidence that what was lost was here all the time and beyond time, nearer than I knew. I realized finally that to continue to indulge in regret was also a subtle form of egotism. The enemy was this very suffering, separate self. Just as I had done years before, I began to sit alone in quiet concentration. But my life was a busier one, more preoccupied with family duties. I sat less intensively and more intermittently than in my youth. For some time I sat occasionally alone. Later, learning of a group of people who sat regularly together in meditation, I joined them.

Then I heard that a Zen center had been started by a small group in Los Angeles. So at last I came to zazen and to the heart of the matter. Sitting in the zendo, listening to Maezumi Roshi read from the ancient texts, I felt my exile was over. I had returned home at last.

I now know that to have had, in any measure, an enlightenment experience is only a beginning. Even to speak of having had it is to risk losing it. Immediacy is surely everything.

To be re-enlightened at every moment, forever, requires eternal vigilance. How can it be otherwise? To continue to practice such awareness at every moment is implicit to the very nature of enlightenment. Thus practice is Reality, Reality-practice. This was the indispensable pillar that had been missing from my life.

Now, like a slowly rising tide, quietly, less dramatically, the timeless vision returns, the infinite possibilities for joyful awareness open at every moment.

To this I now vow to give all my attention.

THE SITTER IN THE FOREST: AN AFTERWORD

My quest for Reality began a little over fifty years ago with a vision of a great whirling spiral of light. Only recently have I realized how deeply that vision affected the course of my life right up to this moment.

I began to understand that vision twenty-five years after it happened, when I met the Zen master Hakuun Yasutani Roshi. I knew at once that he was unlike anyone I had ever seen before. The best way to describe him is to say that he was transparent. He was also an undistinguished-looking old fellow with flap ears who lived simply, wore an old black tam-o'-shanter, and loved marshmallows.

Yasutani Roshi says: "Our buddha nature has the great function of deepening illumination endlessly through practice."

Practice? To Western ears, practice suggests movement, action. In the ensuing years I have come to believe that what he meant is the practice of an absence, especially an absence of movement in the most primary, immediate, and perceptual sense.

At that same time, Yasutani Roshi also recommended that shikantaza, a form of Zen meditation, should be my practice. He went on to say, "Shikantaza is like sitting in the center of a clearing in the forest, knowing that ultimate danger is about to strike, but not knowing what form it will take or from what direction it will come."

Let us look intently at Yasutani Roshi's description of shikantaza. We have gone to the forest to sit, presumably to get away from the distractions of the busy everyday world and into a place conducive to quiet meditation. Instead of the usual description of deep calm and peace, however, he describes a situation of life-threatening danger. One might well imagine that this would be the last way to describe an ideal state of meditation. Yet the Roshi used this state as metaphor for the highest mode of zazen—the practice of enlightenment itself.

I believe he did this because, at the moment of ultimate danger, the tension between peak alertness and profound stillness is stretched to its taut limit. As you sit quietly reading, take a moment to imagine that a shocking sound, totally unexpected and dangerously out of place, is suddenly heard nearby, you are not sure from where. Instantly you come to a peak of alertness, at the same time becoming wholly still, scarcely breathing, barely expending an extra iota of energy. You are ready to act instantly. Ten minutes of this intense awareness can be exhausting, combining the absolute height of tension with the deepest inward stillness, creating the near-perfect set of conditions that may open us to enlightenment.

Now feel yourself to be the sitter in the forest. If your eyes shift even momentarily to the left, danger may strike from the right. Even a flick of the eye may divert your full attention. You are not stirring a muscle. Your bodily tension is at once deeply quiet and relaxed and at the same time in a state of balanced, alert order. With virtually no energy dissipated in movement, it is maximally available to perception. With even the smallest movements of eye and voice stilled, there is no support for thought, no inner dialogue. All inner noise has quieted. Attention, neither narrowed and object-directed, nor diffuse as in sleep, nor distracted by internal noise, is now liberated to seek its true center within and to open without. The field of perception has become maximally open and receptive to Being. In this unmoving pool of perceptual clarity, every event carries primary information and is perfectly processed. In this state of near-perfect order, the most unexpected and unpredictable events are accommodated and integrated to the fullest.

I believe it is right here that the measureless moment of enlightenment comes, if it is to come at all; when attention telescopes to point zero at the center and simultaneously opens to infinity at the periphery. Yet neither center nor periphery remains. As the fourteenth century Tibetan, Longchempa, wrote: "One may well burst out in laughter!"

At this moment, there occurs a 180 degree turn in the center of Being, bringing with it an instant shift of perspective from within finite, partial form to the infinite ground of consciousness itself, in which all things may be seen to unfold with incomparable clarity. I believe this simultaneously two-sided nature of perception to be the linchpin of the enlightenment experience.

Yet what D. T. Suzuki called "the most startling event that can happen in consciousness" is only a beginning. Grandiose descriptions of enlightenment tend to obscure the fact that once this Way of Seeing becomes the natural matrix of everyday experience, its practice is a rather homely affair, requiring a continuous, intimate attention and discipline.

One learns to be generally quiet and deeply relaxed. Then slowly, gently, and without effort, one may learn to release any random, infinitesimal movements of the eyes or throat into a stillness so deep that no eyes, no larynx, seem to be there at all. They have been replaced by total emptiness. Gradually perception sharpens and clarifies. At some point, we may realize how incessant our inner noise and chatter had become. All forms of perception begin to acquire the clarity of the plop of the frog jumping into the quiet pond in the Japanese poet Basho's haiku. Every moment of attention, however seemingly trivial, opens to infinity as the perceptual field becomes ever more articulated and clear, without limit.

So ever present that we seldom recognize it, this primary mode of perception is available to each of us at every waking moment. We can experience it by doing nothing more special than not doing what we spend the better part of our lives doing. We have only to sit quietly, breathing naturally, becoming aware of small eye jumps and sub-vocal dialogue by letting them quiet down. Neither tracking nor following anything, we then open the field of perception to whatever occurs, neither clinging to what has just passed nor anticipating the next event. A bird may fly across the field, a child call, a car starts—that's all, no more. All the principles of Zen practice are embodied in this radically simple attention.

In noiseless silence like this, real practice begins. Deep, fully alert silence is the most wholeness-engendering and holy of states. It is the fallow field in which the seeds of enlightenment flourish. There is literally nothing that cannot be done, and done better, within its nurturing embrace.

I now feel quite sure that when eyes and voice are stilled, one cannot perceive from an egoic perspective. The separate self is a boundary phenomenon, largely embedded in speech and thought. When these subside, the ego gives up its dominance and sinks into a subsidiary role. I believe that, undramatic as this may be, it is the source of the "experience of no self" that is so vividly described throughout the literature of mysticism. So long as we remain an "I" who meditates, or an "I" who aspires to enlightenment, we remain trapped in the age-old contradiction.

With the ego absorbed in this immediate and intimate attention—moment to moment—there is no separate experience of enlightenment, no path, no chasm to be bridged. No longer living in the old way, we are lived. Nothing has been lost. All our skills, strategies, relationships, and memories are available for service to a more harmonious mode of being. Far from becoming special, we become more down-to-earth, direct, natural. We become as little children with everything we have since learned in our pocket. All the energy we previously expended in support of our separate selves is now free to flow in the Tao of working, dancing, laughing, sleeping—just living.

> To study the self is to forget the self.
> To forget the self is to be enlightened by
>   the ten thousand dharmas.
>
> Dogen Zenji, *The Shobogenzo*

17: Meeting Flora Courtois

Hakuun Yasutani

IN THE SUMMER OF 1968, along with Soen Nakagawa Roshi and several others, I made a visit to the Zen Mountain Center at Tassajara Hot Springs, California. Located deep in the mountain wilderness of central California, this zendo is an approximately eight-hour drive northwest from Los Angeles and a four-hour drive south from San Francisco.

Leaving the Zen Center of Los Angeles at 9 A.M. on July 9th and pausing to rest a couple of times, our party arrived at Tassajara a little past six in the evening. During the last two hours of our drive, the car climbed a narrow, precipitous, and sharply curving mountain road, through forest so deep it was difficult to imagine anyone's ever having walked there. From time to time, along the road we caught glimpses of deer and squirrels. In the sky far above, hawks drifted in seemingly motionless circles.

From its highest point at a 5,000-foot level the road then descended down to the 400 or 500-foot level into the secluded Tassajara valley with its natural hot springs, waterfalls and rushing streams, old trees, and stone buildings.

Here, in this valley, Shunryu Suzuki Roshi, who came to San Francisco from Japan in 1959 to give guidance in Zen, established the first Zen mountain retreat in America with the help of his American students and the support of other understanding donors. This mountain temple is called Zenshinji.

Prior to this trip, Flora Courtois had been a founding member of the Zen Center of Los Angeles and had been practicing zazen regularly. It was she who drove us to Tassajara and back to Los Angeles. Because of her kindness, we were able to visit Tassajara without any difficulties, even to enjoy a bath soaking in the hot springs.

Shortly after returning from this trip, I went to New York with Naka-gawa Roshi for the opening ceremonies of the New York zendo, follow-ing which I returned to Los Angeles. A few days later Mrs. Courtois telephoned to ask if she could discuss a personal experience.

It was on a Tuesday morning at 10 o'clock on July 16th that she came to ZCLA, and I listened to her for well over an hour with Maezumi Sensei interpreting. Although not so fully described as in this book, what she told me was essentially the same.

She began with a description of her growing sense of doubt, as a young girl, concerning all things. She went on to tell how she began to confront the question, "What is the ultimate Reality?" while attending college. She recounted her search through the works of many philosophers, of per-sonal visits to several priests and professors, of how all this was in vain and how she was finally referred to the college psychiatrist. But so little serious attention or understanding was given to her problem that she began to feel isolated from the rest of the college community and fell into a vortex of endless searching. She had several vision-like experiences.

These experiences extended over a period of several years until at last one day, sitting alone in her bedroom on the edge of her bed, absent-mindedly gazing at a nearby desk, she experienced an extraordinary event which resolved all her doubt and filled her with inexpressible joy and delight. This was the turning point. As her awareness deepened over the succeeding months, effortlessly all her questions about ultimate reality were resolved, and her entire attitude toward life underwent a radical change. Even her physical health improved, and she rapidly gained needed weight.

However, when she tried to relate what she described as her experi-ence of "Open Vision" to her professors at college or to the college psy-chiatrist, she met such a blank lack of interest and understanding that she finally concluded there was no one to whom she could try to describe this experience with any hope of recognition or appreciation. She then resolved never to speak of it again until she was confident such a person had been found.

For over twenty-five years until our meeting, she had indeed not spoken of it again. She had become a psychologist and writer, actively involved in community life, as well as a busy housewife and mother.

This is a summary of our original talk. Although more than twenty-five years had passed, she vividly recalled every moment. I had carefully watched and observed her as she spoke. Her facial expression was very calm and tender, without harshness; my total impression was of an individual quite natural and serene.

Listening to her talk, I instinctively felt that to test her experience was unnecessary. That experience she had over twenty-five years ago was still vitally alive today. Immediately I verified that the experience was a very clear kensho. At the same time, I recommended to her that she practice shikantaza with diligence. I pointed out that the further one penetrates into the ocean of Buddhadharma, the more one deepens one's realization. So I emphasized the importance of renewing her determination to practice further because our buddha nature has the great function of deepening illumination endlessly through practice.

Although utterly unaware of what Buddhism or Zen was, Flora Courtois attained enlightenment by herself through her unrelenting struggle with the question, "What is Reality?" This is called having no teacher, or enlightenment by oneself alone. This is the same sort of awakening that Shakyamuni Buddha attained as he saw the dawn star on December 8th, two and a half millennia ago.

The true enlightenment of Buddhism is to realize the Original Self. It is common to all true enlightenment regardless of race, country, time, or tradition. Such enlightenment is not at all exclusive to a particular religion. It is quite certain that everyone may awaken as Mrs. Courtois did if only each would pursue wholeheartedly this search for the Original Self. However, due to inadequate faith and effort few attain it.

Throughout the world there must be others who, like Flora Courtois, awaken alone. Unfortunately, it is very difficult for them to meet a qualified teacher who can examine such experiences and verify whether these are genuine or not, or deep or shallow. Consequently a true experience is often buried and unrevealed.

Further, a first awakening is only the beginning of discovering the

Original Self. To deepen and clarify it, to establish its full function in everyday life, requires never-ending practice. Again, it is even more difficult to meet a teacher able to guide one along this path. Therefore, among these rare kensho flowers that bloom alone in the world, many die without bearing fruit.

I sincerely hope that more persons will appear who will resolutely plunge into realizing the Original True Self. Fortunately Zen, which has been directly and accurately transmitted from the Honored One Shakyamuni Buddha, has recently traveled to take root in Western soil.

I urge that you be diligent in your practice, so that you may penetrate to clear awakening and continue to ever deepen your enlightenment.

With firm confidence, I recommend Zen practice, not only so that each of you will find peace and wisdom, but also so that peace and reconciliation for all humanity will follow as a natural consequence.

Appendix
Effort and Intuition:
The Sudden and the Gradual Reconsidered
Neal Donner

T HE GRADUALIST, head monk Yuquan Shenxiu (J. Gyokusen Jinshu) (first in the "Northern School"), said:

> *The body is the Bodhi-tree,*
> *The mind is like a clear mirror.*
> *At all times we must strive to polish it.*
> *And must not let the dust collect.*

The suddenist, illiterate country boy Dajian Huineng (J. Daikan Eno) (first in the "Southern School"), said:

> *Bodhi originally has no tree,*
> *The mirror also has no stand.*
> *Buddha nature is always clean and pure;*
> *(or, "From the first, there is not a single thing.")*
> *Where is there room for dust?*
> (tr. Philip Yampolsky)

One of the best-known stories in Zen is the competition between the above two views. The Fifth Ancestor had asked his disciples to compose verses so that he could judge the depth of their attainment. Shenxiu and Huineng were the only two with the confidence to expose themselves to the Fifth Ancestor's judgment.

This story crystallizes in people's minds the famous contrast between sudden and gradual even if they have never read the Platform Sutra, where the tale is found. While the origins of the controversy can be traced to more than a thousand years before, and its reverberations have continued more than a thousand years to the present, the Platform Sutra itself is the classical, and immensely popular, statement of the sudden-gradual dichotomy.

As those who have heard or read the story know well, Huineng's "sudden enlightenment" verse was judged the more profound and earned him the ancestorship. In consequence, both Rinzai and Soto Zen are said to be descended from him. Very simple, we say to ourselves, and feel we are clear about sudden and gradual. Suddenness is better than gradualness. Obviously.

Only we might wonder how gradualism could have hung on so persistently that it still seems to have the power to challenge suddenness. Perhaps we have heard or read a Zen teacher emphasize the gradual as a necessary complement, not merely the abhorred opposite, of the sudden. Or perhaps we have read or heard discussion in which various meanings of the sudden-gradual dichotomy were illuminated. Or we may have concluded on our own that there is something fishy about such a cut-and-dried opposition. It doesn't seem so simple any more. In fact, it is in part this ambiguity, this richness and pliability of their meanings that has helped to make this pair of words so resoundingly evocative through a millennium of East Asian cultural history. Only a few Western pairs of opposites have had such a prominent career; free will versus determinism comes to mind as one of these.

It is misleading to rely on the Platform Sutra for one's understanding of the sudden-gradual opposition, for as scholars have clearly realized only in this century, that text and the similar pronouncements by Huineng's successors in the Southern School are partisan arguments for the superiority of their approach and lineage over the "Northern School." In fact, Huineng's presumed rival Shenxiu turned out to be an eminent and successful meditation teacher. He and his successors powerfully expounded mainstream Mahayana, and certainly he was far better known in his own lifetime that Huineng. This hints that we must beware of allowing sectarian polemics to hinder us from a clear appreciation of the gradualistic mode of practice. By broadening the focus to include dynamics active in Chinese intellectual and religious history as a whole, we can avoid being caught at one extreme of the controversy.

Beginning at least as early as twenty-five hundred years ago, well before the introduction of Buddhism, China developed two quite different approaches to, as well as definitions of, sagehood. These predate the Platform Sutra by a millennium, but uncannily foretell many elements of the later Buddhist controversy. On the one hand, Confucianism stood for the piece-by-piece accumulation of virtue and discriminating knowledge, an affirmation and continuation of what was best in human tradition. On the other, Taoism recommended a return to the primordial Source, the inexpressible, spontaneous activity of the human mind. The Confucian way was characterized by its opponents as stuffy, formalistic, pedestrian, conventional, and limiting (though they could not deny that it gave to Chinese society a structure and coherence unrivalled in any other land). The Taoist way was considered by its enemies to be undisciplined, anti-intellectual, disrespectful, impulsive, and not quite . sane (though they had to admit that is was, and is, associated with much of the finest of Chinese literature and painting, medieval science and technology, and also with numerous—and often justified—popular uprisings against governmental repression). Yet the virtues of each approach were such that coexistence even in a single person was common and "Confucian in office, Taoist in retirement" a well-known phrase. They seemed to express different but not necessarily antagonistic aspects of the Chinese (or human?) character, rising and falling in their predominance through the lives of individuals and the history of the nation. Even today it is not difficult to discern in China both trends of thought, though now under different names, contending with and influencing each other.

This is part of the matrix from which was drawn the Zen sudden-gradual debate. For many centuries the Confucian bias for measured, rationalistic, gradual improvement had stood in contrast to the Taoist sudden rush of feeling, the intuitive leap, the abandonment to impulse. Entering China in about the second century A.D., Buddhism wavered for five hundred years between these two poles. Zen finally aligned itself on the side of suddenness (though without suppressing many of the "gradual" virtues). Other Chinese Buddhist schools took their places elsewhere on the spectrum. The issue was also joined, though never at the forefront of debate, in Indian Buddhism, before any passage to China. Earlier forms of Buddhism had seen "craving" (desire) as the fundamental obstruction on the Path, and recommended a variety of gradualistic disciplines to overcome this as well as the related emotional defilements. While they plainly held that "wrong views" or intellectual defilements also needed rectifying, the early Buddhists had not yet identified dualism as the prime delusion.

Then in the first century B.C., the great sutras on the perfection of wisdom began to clarify the deeper sense of "wrong view": as the delusion that involves taking as ultimates the discriminations we make with our minds. This discrimination is what is meant by "dualism." The mind fulfills its proper function when it analyzes, discriminates, separates, and distinguishes. But it errs if it understands the resultant fragmentation of reality to be more real than the prior interconnectedness.

Mahayana Buddhism maintains craving can only arise out of this ignorance of the real nature of ourselves and the objects we crave. Meditation functions then to bring us back to our senses, as it were, including the intuitive sense that involves direct experience of the world, unmediated by the discriminating mind or its servant, language. To this end, one must see *through* every distinction made by the mind, in particular the seductively self-evident oppositions between self and other, past and future, and even ignorance and enlightenment. The point is not to call such concepts false. It is rather to open the way to a deeper awareness of what they signify and how they relate to each other. The concept of "emptiness," and its experiential realization in meditation, do, however, deprive of ultimate support every pair of antonyms in the Buddhist, or any, vocabulary.

Then even ignorance and enlightenment are not truly to be opposed to each other, being in some sense identical. Certain Mahayana sutras very powerfully make the point that, even in our ignorance, we are fundamentally already enlightened buddhas. In short, we all have a buddha nature. Many shades of emphasis are possible here, but roughly speaking, this is the doctrinal background in Indian Mahayana Buddhism which enabled Huineng to win the poetry contest while remaining faithful to the Mahayana tradition. The enlightened sage, monk or nun, or buddha, is able to see the identity between dust and mirror, between defilements and the (enlightened) mind. In fact the moment when she realizes this is the same moment when she becomes enlightened, suddenly.

Now in India such radical implications of the doctrine of emptiness were seldom emphasized, and more than in China, the great treatises and teachers preferred to expound a gradual attainment of the goal. Late in the eighth century, when Tibet was still in the early stages of conversion to Buddhism, both the Indian and the Chinese approaches contended there for dominance. The gradualistic Indian way emerged the victor, but the records which have remained of the debate in Tibet are, along with the nearly contemporaneous Northern and Southern School Zen materials, among the best evidence we have of the meanings associated with "sudden" and "gradual" in the minds of practicing Chinese Buddhist monks in the eighth century. Ironically, the monk who represented the "sudden" Chinese side of the debate seems to have been in Shenxiu's Northern ("gradual") lineage. The gradualistic Indian party turns out to have been much more "gradual" than either side in the purely Chinese Northern-and-Southern debate.

Sudden-and-gradual exercised the minds of influential Chinese Buddhists even before Zen arose. Interest first developed in the sudden *teaching*, the nothing-held-back ultimate exposition of the Buddha, with no concession made to those of weak ability to comprehend. (This "sudden teaching" has a different sense from the "teaching of sudden enlightenment" contained in works like the Platform Sutra.) Then somewhat later the expression "sudden *practice*" was used to indicate the mode of contemplation where the meditator from the outset focused his awareness on the highest truth, omitting preparatory exercises. Gradual teaching and gradual practice are easily understood by reference to these. But these meanings of sudden-and-gradual were not an important part of the later controversies.

Even without a historical context, or knowledge of positions historically advocated by various monks and thinkers, the famous poem contest creates for us a vivid picture of the alternatives. "Sudden" seems to mean that the (inherently enlightened) mind is incapable of being defiled. However, the Southern School emphatically denounces those who hold to the contrary, that is, who think the mind *can* be defiled—so evidently there still exist humans as yet unenlightened (despite the fact that their minds cannot be defiled). Clearly such suddenists admit that there is a moment in the life of individuals when a further step is taken, namely to *realize* what is already true, and it is this which is sudden and abrupt. In fact, the writings of the Southern School often seem to suggest that a single experience of this kind is enough to turn us into enlightened buddhas.

Whatever the polemics in any given situation may have been, the sentence preceding this one was not the considered position of mainstream Zen for any length of time. The popular understanding may perhaps have been another matter. But it is important for us not to be misled by the apparent simplicity of the opposing ideas, no matter how charming we find the possibility of sudden attainment.

It is true that the Southern School tended not to emphasize it, but even they accorded a place to gradualism. Only for them, gradual spiritual cultivation was a stage that *followed* an initial "sudden" enlightenment. The Southern School preferred not to emphasize whatever preparatory training preceeded this, focusing instead on an initial moment when the mists of delusion are first penetrated. However, there was still supposed to ensue a long period of gradual practice, interspersed with further enlightenment experiences of various depths, before the final stage of buddhahood was reached. And while some of the texts and passages of Southern School figures blur the distinction between the initial awakening and the final realization, there is no sustained insistence on their identity. This alerts us to the ambiguity of the word "enlightenment." We find it used for the entire range of insight experiences and levels of accomplishment, from first to last, in Asian languages as well as in English. It is even used to refer to the worldings in their *un*enlightened state, since these too are inherently buddhas, already having the buddha nature.

Now since all later Zen masters claimed descent from the Southern School, their slogan of sudden enlightenment reached the status of a dogma. A few generations after the Platform Sutra, the great ninth century Zen and Huayen master Guifeng Zongmi (J. Keiho Shumitsu) set forth what became the classical interpretation. Zongmi placed "sudden enlightenment" unambiguously at the *beginning* of the spiritual quest, to be followed by numerous stages of realization reached through sometimes arduous gradualistic spiritual cultivation (involving zazen first and foremost). Buddhahood, i.e. unsurpassed, supreme enlightenment, lay at the end of this process. Since Zongmi also specifically allowed for inherent buddha nature in all beings, no matter how deluded, he preserved the tradition that we are all enlightened already (but only have to realize it). This greatly clarified the whole issue, for the word "enlightenment" could now be used without confusion in three distinct senses: (1) inherent buddha nature, (2) initial opening (as well as further intermediate openings), and (3) buddhahood. Each could be called sudden, though inherent buddha nature is "sudden" in a way different from the others (not preceded, that is, by an earlier and lower stage). But the term "sudden enlightenment" had its own value as a slogan, so it was reserved for the second sense, the initial awakening, while the process following it and leading up to buddhahood was carefully termed "gradual cultivation" (instead of "gradual enlightenment," even though it clearly involved a continuous ascent to higher levels of wisdom).

In Zen as in other schools of Buddhism, from time to time a tendency arose to completely equate the first sense, inherent buddha nature with the third, full buddhahood. This led to a denial of the necessity of practice, and even to the praise of questionable moral behavior as the essence of the Way. The anything-goes mentality found comfort in the abolition of distinctions.

The Southern School's attack on the presumed gradualism of the Northern School (Shenxiu and the other dust-wipers) was so successful that no later Zen lineage remained willing to characterize itself as "gradualist." Chinese Buddhism had been leaning further and further away from "gradualism" for centuries, long before Zen arose. Gradual attainment had seemed to the Chinese to involve a dualism, precisely the root delusion that practice was meant to overcome. So a tendency arose to speak as much as possible from the ultimate standpoint (where dualisms are transcended), rather than the relative (where dualisms are in force). The Southern complaint against the Northerners thus amounted to the accusation that they were unaware of the ultimate standpoint, being completely stuck in dualism.

Historical research in the twentieth century demonstrated that the Southern characterization of the Northern School was less than accurate. Far from being dualistic, the Northern School not only acknowledged buddha nature in all beings (as in Zongmi's first sense), but also taught the instantaneous attainment of supreme wisdom (Zongmi's third sense, buddhahood). The difference between the two schools was one of emphasis, even style, rather than substance. The Southerners hardly mentioned the need for practice, preferring to focus on what Zongmi later defined as the initial enlightenment experience. They declined, until the time of Zongmi himself (as spiritual heir to this transmission), to go into any detail about the central practice of meditation, but did not allow for gradual cultivation (which implicitly corresponded to a gradual enlightenment). It is a historical irony that certain teachers in the early Zen ("meditation") school maintained such a reluctance to teach carefully the process of meditation.

On the other hand, the Northerners preferred to emphasize the necessity of gradual cultivation, unremitting effort in meditation, and constant application. It is true that they made distinctions among the various sorts of karmic obstacles, instead of concentrating exclusively on the root delusion, dualistic thinking. But they accepted that the final enlightenment experience itself, following upon gradual cultivation, was sudden.

In short, while the Southerners held to *sudden enlightenment* followed by gradual cultivation, the Northerners held to *gradual cultivation* followed by sudden enlightenment. The main Southern innovation seems to have been this emphasis on the initial opening, downplaying, but not consistently denying, the necessity of the practice of sitting meditation. Neither buddha nature, nor its inherence in all beings, was a new assertion made by Southern Zen—both of these ideas dated from centuries before. But that one's initial view of it is so abrupt—*this* had never yet been emphasized so strongly.

We understand today that the "Northern and Southern Schools" controversies bore a political significance over and above the overt clash of doctrines or styles of practice. Those who marched under the banner of sudden enlightenment can be seen as in rebellion against the religious establishment, itself represented by the likes of Shenxiu. This monk, basking in imperial favor, was a consummate technician of religious practice, a professional meditator and the National Teacher of the realm. He and his disciples stood for a sort of Zen that could be mastered, like a craft, by the rational expenditure of effort. In contrast, the Southerners daringly asserted the primacy of intuition, opening thereby even to comparative amateurs the way to enlightenment (although a closer look discloses that the initial intuitive opening was more often what they meant than buddhahood in the full sense). Finally, Shenxiu's teachings and disciples were toppled from their regal place of eminence and, at the end of the eighth century, the leader of the insurgent intuitionists was posthumously declared seventh ancestor, the legitimate successor of Huineng. Perhaps as if to emphasize their distance from such political considerations, the Soto and Rinzai lines of Zen trace their lineages through two *other* seventh ancestors, also disciples of Huineng, but obscure compared to this leader of the Southern School.

Such an interpretation of the sudden-gradual controversy (while it constitutes only one of the dimensions involved) seems to make even more sense when juxtaposed with certain trends in Chinese literature and art criticism. Four hundred years ago the influential "theory of the Southern and Northern Schools" was formulated. This was a method of classifying all Chinese landscape painting that cast the "suddenists" as intuitive amateurs, even inspired rebels, while the "gradualists" were comprised of the stuffy professionals who had developed their skills by sustained application. Thus one type of painter was spontaneous, the other mannered. While these categories fail to correspond to social groupings, they do disclose the values popular among Chinese viewers of Chinese art.

In the realm of literature a similar phenomenon can be found. Already by the thirteenth century a distinction had been made between "sudden" and "gradual" in the composition of poetry. Here the term "suddenist" refers to the type of poet who loved to flout conventions, wrote spontaneously and intuitively, gained his daily bread by other means than writing, and hailed from the provinces. The "gradualist" bore a higher regard for rules and tradition, and was a professional who typically dwelt in the capital.

In poetry and landscape painting, just as in Zen itself, no degree of reverence for intuition could finally expunge the need for discipline.

Intuition was given a certain primacy, in art as in religion, yet painstaking effort was also seen in these traditions to be a necessary component of the creative or religious life. The point was not to choose between extremes, but to resolve the question of how to harmonize or transcend them.

Many solutions were proposed to this dilemma or antinomy in art criticism, literature, Zen, Chinese Buddhism as a whole, and even Neo-Confucianism. The great Zen master Dogen (thirteenth century) developed the classical Japanese Soto Zen view of the relationship between the poles of sudden and gradual. Though his stress on practice has led some modern scholars to tag him as "gradual," he took great pains to distinguish his views from those who saw themselves as having to achieve a buddhahood beyond their natural state. And while his stress on the inherent buddhahood of all beings has led others to claim him for the "sudden" camp, still he carefully avoided (indeed condemned) those denials of practice to which the most extreme suddenists had on occasion resorted. Dogen's celebrated doctrine of the identity of practice and realization preserves both path and goal in a manner parallel to the distinction Zongmi had made between the various uses of the term "enlightenment."

For Dogen, "sudden enlightenment" neither precedes nor follows "gradual cultivation": Dogen prefers to speak instead of the role of practice in making manifest the (unmanifested) inherent buddhahood which we each possess. But the fact of enlightenment being inherent from the first never cancels out the need for committed practice, nor must frequent sitting suggest to the meditator that he is incomplete (i.e. must yet acquire buddhahood). Practice does not *create* enlightenment then, but *actualizes* an inherent, pre-existing potentiality. Without practice, this actualization of potential fails to occur.

The record shows that "gradual" is part of, as well as often the name of, an idea cluster that includes notions like "relative," "dualistic," "incomplete," "establishmentarian," and "disciplined." Similarly, "sudden" associates with "absolute," "nondual," "perfected," "unconventional," and "impulsive." Seldom, if ever, were all possible associated meanings intended—or even intelligible—in a given usage of one term of the famous pair. But for those of us involved in practice more than theory, sudden-gradual reduces largely to the contrast between our intuition and our effort. The various strands of Zen tradition finally agree that insight may occur abruptly, but also that without disciplined intention, such insight is likely either not to arrive, or once present, to dissipate by force of our other experiences and habits.

With or without a teacher then, we each are left with the task of integrating our "sudden" aspect (letting go into our inherently perfect intuition) with our "gradual" aspect (striving effortfully). As we wrestle with this apparent paradox of "willing to be spontaneous," we find that the historical clash of opposing doctrines yields to the specific details of our personal practice. These comprise, for each of us, a region that eludes the prying eyes of scholars.

Glossary

Amitabha (Skt; J. Amida): The Buddha of Infinite Light, whose forty-eight vows epitomize the bodhisattva spirit of boundless compassion. According to Shin Buddhists, anyone who calls upon Amitabha's name with deep faith will be reborn in the Western paradise, the Pure Land, where Amitabha is said to reside.

Ancestor: Strictly speaking, the first thirty-four Dharma successors from Shakyamuni Buddha through the Sixth Chinese Ancestor, Huineng (J. Eno, 638–713). More generally, an honorific term used to describe deceased Zen masters of outstanding attainment.

ango (J) (lit. "peaceful dwelling"): A practice period, usually three months in length, devoted to meditation, study, and communal work.

anuttara samyak sambodhi (Skt): Literally, supreme perfect enlightenment.

Avalokitesvara (Skt; J. Kannon, Kanzeon, Kanjizai): One of the principal bodhisattvas in the Zen Buddhist tradition, Avalokitesvara is the embodiment of great compassion and is often represented in the female form.

Avatamsaka Sutra (Skt; Ch. *Huayan;* J. *Kegonkyo*) (lit. "garland sutra," also translated as "Flower Ornament Sutra"): Said to be the teachings of Shakyamuni Buddha during the three weeks immediately following his great enlightenment, the Avatamsaka Sutra teaches the mutual interdependence and interpenetration of all phenomena and is the basic text of the Hua-yan school.

Blue Cliff Record (Ch. *Biyan lu;* J. *Hekiganroku*): A collection of one hundred koans compiled, with appreciatory verses, by Master Xuedou

Chongxian (J. Setcho Juken, 980–1052) and with commentaries by Master Yuanwu Keqin (J. Engo Kokugon, 1063–1135). A text of fundamental importance for koan study in the Rinzai school, the *Blue Cliff Record* was also studied by Dogen Zenji, who brought back a handwritten copy when he returned to Japan from China.

bodhi mandala (Skt): Refers to the place of enlightenment, which has no particular location but is seen everywhere by the penetrating eye of prajna wisdom.

bodhi-mind: The mind in which an aspiration to enlightenment has been awakened.

Bodhidharma (Skt; J. Daruma, d. 532 C.E.): Known as the First Ch'an Ancestor in China, Bodhidharma was the Indian master who brought Zen to China. According to tradition he sat in a cave doing zazen for nine years before transmitting the Dharma to Huike (J. Eka), the Second Ancestor (*Gateless Gate*, Case 41). Attributed to Bodhidharma is the famous four-line verse characterizing Zen: *A special transmission outside the scriptures. No dependence on words and letters. Seeing directly into the mind. Realizing true nature, becoming Buddha.*

bodhisattva (Skt) (lit. "enlightenment being"): One who practices the Buddha Way and compassionately forgoes final enlightenment for the sake of helping others become enlightened. The exemplar in Mahayana Buddhism.

Book of Equanimity (Ch. *Congrong lu;* J. *Shoyoroku;* English title also translated as *Book of Serenity*): A collection of one hundred koans following the pattern of the *Blue Cliff Record*, compiled, with appreciatory verses, by Master Tiantong Hongzhi (J. Tendo Wanshi, 1091–1157). In 1223, Master Wansong Xingxiu (J. Bansho Gyoshu, 1166–1246) added commentaries and capping phrases. The *Book of Equanimity* is widely used in the Soto school and is known as a work of great depth and subtlety.

bosatsukai (J) (lit. "a meeting of bodhisattvas"): Can be used to refer to any group of Zen Buddhists who meet together for practice.

Buddha (lit. "awakened one"): The historical Buddha Shakyamuni.

buddha: Persons who have attained buddhahood; the essential truth, the true nature of all beings. *See also* buddha nature.

buddhadharma (J. buppo): Buddhist teachings.

buddha nature: The intrinsic nature of all beings; true nature, true self, ultimate reality.

Buddha Way (J. butsudo): The Way taught by Shakyamuni Buddha.

buji Zen (J) (lit. "no-matter" Zen): An excessively casual attitude toward Zen discipline and training, based on the rationalization that since we are all fundamentally buddhas, we need not bother with practice, morality, or realization.

capping phrase (J. jakugo): A pithy expression which concisely summarizes or comments upon part or all of a koan. Zen students who work with koans are traditionally required to present capping phrases as further evidence of their understanding.

compassion (Skt. karuna): This aspect of practice is emphasized in Mahayana Buddhism, especially in the precepts and the vow to save all sentient beings. Compassion is the natural outgrowth of prajna wisdom; the two invariably go hand in hand.

Dharma (Skt): The teachings of the Buddha; Truth; Buddhist doctrine; universal Law. *See also* dharmas.

Dharma combat (or Dharma dialogue): Lively interchange in which two Zen students, or student and teacher, test and sharpen their understanding.

Dharma hall: A room or building in a practice center in which Dharma talks are given.

Dharma name: The name given to someone upon receiving the precepts (jukai), thus formally becoming a Buddhist.

Dharma successor: A person deemed worthy by a Zen teacher to carry on the teaching lineage and authorized to teach Zen.

Dharma transmission: Designation of a person as a Dharma successor. *See also* inka, shiho.

Dharmakaya (Skt; J. hosshin): One aspect of the threefold body of Buddha; the Absolute beyond all discrimination.

dharmas (Skt): Phenomena; elements or constituents of existence.

dhyana (Skt): Similar in meaning to samadhi. In early Buddhism, the term referred to various stages of concentrated awareness. Its Chinese and Japanese equivalents (Ch'an and Zen, respectively) have broader implications.

Diamond Sutra (Skt. *Vajracchedika Sutra;* J. *Kongokyo*): Highly regarded by the Zen sect, it sets forth the doctrines of sunyata and prajna. The Sixth Ancestor attained enlightenment upon hearing a phrase from this sutra.

Dogen Kigen Zenji (1200–1253): Co-founder of the Japanese Soto school of Zen, Dogen Zenji established Eiheiji, a principal Soto training monastery, and is best known for his collection of Dharma essays, *Shobogenzo.*

dojo (J): A training center.

dokusan (J): A one-to-one encounter between Zen student and Zen teacher in which the student's understanding is probed and stimulated and in which the student may consult the teacher on any matters arising directly out of practice.

Dongshan Liangjie (Ch; J. Tozan Ryokai, 807–869): Principal founder of the Chinese Soto school. Famous for setting forth the teaching of the Five Positions (J. Goi) and for his poem *Baojing sanmei* (J. *Hokkyozammai* [Most Excellent Mirror Wisdom Samadhi]).

Eightfold Path: The fourth Noble Truth, in which Shakyamuni Buddha indicated the Way to put an end to suffering. The Eightfold Path consists of: right views, right thought, right speech, right action, right livelihood, right effort, right mindfulness, and right samadhi.

Eiheiji: One of the two main training monasteries of the Soto school of Zen, founded by Dogen Zenji in 1243. While the Chinese characters literally mean "temple of eternal peace," they are also a reference to the era when Buddhism was believed to have been first introduced to China.

emptiness (Skt. sunyata; J. ku): The fundamental nature of all phenomena.

enlightenment: Realization of one's true nature.

five desires: 1. Money or wealth; 2. material things, including sex; 3. food; 4. fame; and 5. sleep. Also rendered as greed, lust, fame, gluttony, and laziness.

Four Noble Truths: A fundamental teaching of the Buddha concerning the nature of life and the Way of Buddhist practice. It states that: 1) there is suffering; 2) suffering has a cause; 3) there is a way to put an end to the cause of suffering; 4) the way to end suffering is the Eightfold Path.

Four Vows: Zen students chant these four great bodhisattva vows daily as an expression of their aspiration: "Sentient beings are numberless; I vow to save them. Desires are inexhaustible; I vow to put an end to them. The Dharmas are boundless; I vow to master them. The Buddha Way is unsurpassable; I vow to attain it."

Fukanzazengi (J) (lit. "Universal Promotion of the Principles of Zazen"): A meditation manual by Dogen Zenji.

Fusatsu (J; Skt. uposatha): A ceremony, dating back to the time of the historical Buddha, for atonement and renewing the vows.

Gakki (J): Memorial service.

Genjokoan (J) (lit: "realization of ultimate reality"): One of the key chapters of Dogen Zenji's *Shobogenzo* and a seminal essay in Japanese Soto Zen, it explores with great subtlety the relationship between practice and realization; the enlightenment of everyday life.

Great Death: The point in deep samadhi where all sense of self and other, one and many, falls away. Immediately following Great Death is Great Rebirth, or great enlightenment.

Great Rebirth: Great enlightenment.

Hakuin Ekaku Zenji (1686–1769): The first Ancestor of Japanese Rinzai Zen, through whom all present-day Rinzai masters have their lineage. He systematized koan study as we know it today.

hara (J): The area of the lower abdomen which is the physical center of gravity of the human body, and which becomes a center of awareness in zazen.

Heart Sutra (Skt. *Prajnaparamita hridaya sutra; J. Hannya haramita shingyo*): The essence of the Prajnaparamita literature succinctly expressed in one page. Chanted daily in Zen temples everywhere, its central teaching is "form is emptiness, emptiness is form."

Hotei (J; Ch. Budai): The happy, big-bellied bodhisattva often depicted with a large sack on his back and regarded as an incarnation of Maitreya.

inka (J) (lit. "seal of approval"): The seal of approval given to highly accomplished Dharma successors.

joriki (J) (lit. "self-power"): The vital, stabilizing energy arising from strong zazen practice.

jukai (J): Ceremony of receiving the precepts. A person receiving the precepts formally becomes a Buddhist and is given a Dharma name and lineage chart.

kalpa (Skt): An eon; an extremely long period of time.

Kanzeon: See Avalokitesvara.

karma (Skt): The principle of causality, which holds that for every effect there is a cause.

Keizan Jokin Zenji (1268–1325): Fourth Ancestor and co-founder, with his predecessor Dogen Zenji, of the Soto school in Japan. Keizan Zenji was largely responsible for the spread of Japanese Soto Zen.

kensho (J) (lit. "seeing true nature"): An experience of enlightenment; also known as satori.

kinhin (J): Walking zazen.

koan (J): A teaching story recording an exchange between master and student or a master's enlightenment experience. Koans, which may include an everyday life experience, are used in Zen to bring a student to realization and to help clarify enlightenment.

koan study: The intensive inquiry into koans in Zen meditation. Conventional, discursive thinking is bypassed, and a student is encouraged to give spontaneous, direct responses that express the heart of the matter in question. Koan practice helps a student learn the structure of the Dharma and awakens and sharpens the prajna eye, thereby leading to a deep personal transformation.

kyosaku (J) (lit. "waking stick"): A long stick, generally flattened at one end, the kyosaku is carried in the meditation hall by a monitor who periodically strikes sitters on the shoulders to encourage them or to help them stay awake.

Linji Yixuan (J. Rinzai Gigen, d. 867): One of the great masters of the Tang dynasty in China and founder of the Linji school of Zen. Famous for his blows and shouts, Linji is a Dharma successor of Huangbo Xiyun (J. Obaku Kiun).

Lotus Sutra (Sutra of the Lotus of the Wonderful Law) (Skt. *Saddharma pundarika sutra;* J. *Myohorengekyo*): An elaborate presentation, in prose and verse, of the Buddha's teaching that there is fundamentally only one vehicle to liberation and that all beings are able to attain perfect enlightenment. The basic text of the Tendai and Nichiren sects.

makyo (J) (lit. "obstructing demons"): Illusions, fantasies, hallucinations; more generally, any phenomena or experiences, including even enlightenment experiences, which distract one from practice or to which one becomes attached.

Mahaparinirvana Sutra: Mahayana scripture said to be the sermon preached by the Buddha just before his death; not to be confused with the Theravada *Mahaparinibbana Suttanta* of the Pali Canon, which deals with the last days and death of Shakyamuni. *See also* parinirvana.

Mahayana (Skt) (lit. "great vehicle"): Refers to the type of Buddhism found throughout Tibet, China, Korea, Japan, and Vietnam. It emphasizes compassion and the bodhisattva ideal of forgoing final nirvana to remain in the realm of birth and death to help suffering sentient beings.

mandala: A diagrammatic representation of the universe.

Manjusri (Skt; J. Monju): The bodhisattva of wisdom, often depicted riding a lion and holding the sword of non-wisdom and the Prajnaparamita Sutra. Manjusri Bodhisattva is the principal figure on the zendo altar. *See also* Avalokitesvara, Samantabhadra.

Mu (J): The character *mu,* a negative particle which is used to point directly at reality and has no discursive content. The use of the word in this sense originated with Master Zhaozhou Congshen (J. Joshu Jushin, 778–897) who, when asked by a monk, "Does a dog have buddha nature?" answered "Mu!" This incident is the first koan in the *Gateless Gate* and is often the first koan encountered by Zen students. The term *mu* is often used as a synonym of *emptiness,* as is the word "*No.*"

nirvana (Skt; J. nehan): Literally "extinction." In Zen practice, a non-dualistic state beyond life and death.

oryoki (J) (lit. "that which holds just enough"): The nested set of eating bowls given every monk and nun at ordination. Strictly speaking, the term refers exclusively to the largest of these bowls. In early Buddhist tradition, the bowl used in alms rounds by monks and nuns.

paramitas (Skt) (lit. "gone to the other shore"): The six practices of a bodhisattva: giving *(dana);* precepts or morality *(sila);* forbearance *(kshanti);* effort or vigor *(virya);* meditation *(dhyana);* and wisdom *(prajna).*

parinirvana (Skt) (lit. "ultimate nirvana"): Refers to the dissolution of the five skandhas at the death of an enlightened being. *See also* nirvana.

Patriarch: See Ancestor. (Modern usage avoids gender-specific terminology.)

prajna (Skt; J. hannya): Non-dual wisdom.

precepts (Skt. sila; J. kai): Teachings regarding personal conduct, which can be appreciated on a fairly literal level as ethical guidelines and more broadly as aspects of reality itself.

rakusu (J): Made of five strips of cloth, and thus the smallest of the Buddhist robes *(kesa)*, the rakusu is the only kesa worn by both monks and laypersons and is suspended from the neck by a cloth halter.

Rinzai Gigen: See Linji Yixuan.

Rinzai school: The Zen lineage founded by Master Linji Yixuan (J. Rinzai Gigen, d. 867).

Roshi (J) (lit. "old teacher"): An term used to refer to a senior Zen teacher.

samadhi (Skt; J. zammai): A state of mind characterized by one-pointedness of attention. More broadly, any of numerous meditative states.

Samantabhadra (Skt; J. Fugen): One of the three principal bodhisattvas in the Zen Buddhist tradition, Samantabhadra is associated with compassionate action. *See also* Avalokitesvara, Manjusri.

samu (J): Working zazen, often physical labor.

Sangha (Skt): Originally the community of Buddhist monks and nuns, the term sangha later came to include laypersons as well. The harmonious interrelationship of all beings, phenomena, and events.

sanzen (J) (lit. "penetration [in] Zen"): In the Rinzai tradition, sanzen is synonymous with dokusan. For Dogen Zenji, founder of the Soto school in Japan, however, sanzen more broadly signifies the proper practice of zazen.

satori: See kensho.

sesshin (lit. "unified mind"): A time for intensive Zen practice, usually lasting one to seven days.

Shakyamuni (Skt) (lit "the Silent Sage of the Shakya Clan"): The title used to refer to Siddhartha Gautama, the historical Buddha, after his enlightenment.

shiho (J): Dharma transmission.

shikantaza (J) (lit. "just sitting"): The zazen of intense, non-discursive awareness; "zazen doing zazen."

Shobogenzo (J) (lit. "Treasury of the True Dharma Eye"): Masterwork of Dogen Zenji, founder of the Japanese Soto Zen school, it comprises some ninety-five essays generally considered to be one of the most subtle and profound works in religious literature.

shobogenzo nehan myoshin (J) (lit. "treasury of the true Dharma eye, subtle mind of nirvana"): This phrase, attributed to the Buddha upon his transmission of the Dharma to Mahakasyapa, expresses the essence of Dharma transmission in which the minds of master and disciple become one.

shosan (J): A formal meeting in which a Zen teacher gives a short talk and then engages in a dialogue with students. *See also* Dharma combat.

Sixth Ancestor Huineng (J. Eno, 638–713): Traditionally said to be illiterate, Huineng was enlightened while still a layperson upon hearing a recitation of the Diamond Sutra. His teaching, as recorded in the Platform Sutra, stresses "sudden enlightenment" and the identity of meditation *(dhyana)* and wisdom *(prajna)*. All lines of Zen now extant descend from him.

skandhas (Skt) (lit. "heaps, aggregates"): In Buddhist psychology, the five elements which collectively give rise to the illusion of self. They are: form, sensation, conception, discrimination, and awareness.

Sojiji: One of the two main monasteries of the Soto Zen school, founded in 1321 by Keizan Zenji.

Soto school: The Zen lineage founded in China by Masters Dongshan Liangjie (J. Tozan Ryokai, 807–869) and Caoshan Benji (J. Sozan Honjaku, 840–901). The Japanese branch was founded by Masters Dogen Kigen (1200–1253) and Keizan Jokin (1268–1325).

Sunyata: See emptiness.

sutra (Skt) (lit. "thread"): Buddhist scripture; a dialogue or sermon attributed to the Buddha.

tanto (J): The person in charge of the operations of a zendo.

Tathagata (Skt; J. Nyorai): The name the Buddha used in referring to himself; literally means "thus-come."

teisho (J): A formal commentary by a Zen master on a koan or other Zen text. In its strictest sense, teisho is non-dualistic and is thus distinguished from a Dharma talk, which is a lecture on a Buddhist topic.

ten directions: The four cardinal directions, the four points in between, and up and down.

Ten Ox-herding Pictures: Of Chinese origin, they represent in verse and pictures a step-by-step guide to the bodhisattva path.

Ten Realms: The realms of buddhas, bodhisattvas, pratyeka-buddhas, sravaka-buddhas, heavenly beings, human beings, fighting spirits, animals, hungry ghosts, and hell-dwellers.

tenzo (J): Head cook in a monastery or Zen center; considered to be one of the most challenging assignments.

three poisons: Greed, aggression, and ignorance.

three times: Past, present, and future.

Three Treasures (J. sambo): Buddha, Dharma, and Sangha.

three worlds: 1) The worlds of desire, form, and formlessness. 2) Past, present, and future.

tokudo (J.): Ceremony of receiving the precepts. There are two kinds of tokudo: *zaike* (householder) tokudo, in which one formally becomes a lay Buddhist; and *shukke* (home departure) tokudo, in which one becomes a monk or a nun.

Vinaya (Skt) (lit. "discipline"): The code of monastic conduct.

Wansong Xingxiu (Ch; J. Bansho Gyoshu, 1166–1246): Chinese Soto Zen master who added commentaries and capping phrases to the 100 koans collected by Hongzhi Zengjue (Tiantong) (J. Tendo Wanshi) in the *Book of Equanimity* (Ch. *Congrong lu;* J. *Shoyoroku*).

Yanyang Shanxin (Ch; J. Genyo Zenshin, n.d.). Disciple of Zhaozhou Congshen.

Yunmen Wenyan (Ch; J. Ummon Bun'en, 863–949): Founder of the Yunmen (J. Ummon) school, later absorbed into the Linji (J. Rinzai) school. He was known for his mastery of verbal expression.

zafu (J) (lit. "sitting cushion"): Round cushion used for zazen.

zazen (J) (lit. "sitting meditation"): The practice of Zen meditation.

zendo (J): A place set aside for the practice of zazen.

zenji (J) (lit. "Zen master"): An honorific term used to refer to a master of high rank or outstanding attainment, most notably for the abbots of Eiheiji and Sojiji, the head training monasteries of the Japanese Soto School.

Zhaozhou Congshen (Ch; J. Joshu Jushin, 778–897): One of the greatest masters of the Tang dynasty, the golden age of Zen. Zhaozhou became a disciple of Master Nanquan at the age of eighteen and continued to practice zazen for over one hundred years. He appears frequently in koans and is especially famous for the koan "Zhaozhou's Dog." *See also* mu.

Chinese-Japanese Name Glossary

JAPANESE—CHINESE

Bansho Gyoshu	Wansang Xingxiu
Bokushu Domyo	Muzhou Daoming
Daie Soko	Dahui Zonggao
Daikan Eno	Huineng Dajian
Daiman Konin	Daman Hongren
Engo Kokugon	Yuanwu Keqin
Genyo Zenshin	Yanyang Shanxin
Gyokusen Jinshu	Yuquan Shenxiu
Joshu Jushin	Zhaozhou Congshen
Keiho Shumitsu	Guifeng Zongmi
Mumon Ekai	Wumen Huikai
Obaku Kiun	Huangbo Xiyun
Rinzai Gigen	Linji Yixuan
Seigen Isshin	Qingyuan Weihsin
Sekiso Keisho	Shishuang Qingzhu
Sekito Kisen	Shitou Xiqian
Seppo Gison	Xuefeng Yicun
Setcho Juken	Xuedou Chongxian
Sozan Honjaku	Caoshan Benji
Taiso Eka	Daizu Huike
Tozan Ryokai	Dongshan Liangjie
Ummon Bun'en	Yunmen Wenyan
Ungo Doyo	Yunju Daoying
Wanshi Shogaku	Hongzhi Zengjue (Tiantong)

Index

About the Authors

HAKUYU TAIZAN MAEZUMI ROSHI (1931–1995) A Soto Zen priest, Maezumi Roshi was a successor to masters representing three major lines of Zen teachings: the Soto Zen lineages of Hakujun Kuroda Roshi and Hakuun Yasutani Roshi, and the Rinzai Zen lineage of Koryu Osaka Roshi. He was the founding abbot and resident Zen master of the Zen Center of Los Angeles, and Zen Mountain Center, and the founder of the White Plum lineage. He was co-author, with Bernie Tetsugen Glassman, of *The Way of Everyday Life* (Los Angeles: Zen Center of Los Angeles Publications, 1978) and *On Zen Practice* (Boston: Wisdom Publications, 2002), and author of *The Echoless Valley* (Mt. Tremper, N.Y.: Dharma Communications, 1998), *Teaching of the Great Mountain* (edited by Anton Tenkei Coppens, Boston: Tuttle, 2001), and *Appreciate Your Life: The Essence of Zen Practice* (edited by Wendy Egyoku Nakao and Eve Myonen Marko, Boston: Shambhala, 2001).

BERNIE TETSUGEN GLASSMAN ROSHI (1939–) Maezumi Roshi's first Dharma successor, Glassman Roshi is the founder of the Greyston Foundation, and cofounder with his late wife, Sandra Jishu Holmes Roshi, of the Peacemaker Community. He is the co-author, with Rick Fields, of *Instructions to the Cook* (New York: Bell Tower, 1996) and the author of *Bearing Witness* (New York: Bell Tower, 1998) and *Infinite Circle* (Shambhala: Boston, 2002). He lives in Massachusetts.

FLORA COURTOIS (1916–2000) Flora Courtois was a psychologist and early brain biofeedback researcher. A founding member of Zen Center of Los Angeles, she authored a small book, *An Experience of Enlightenment,* and numerous articles about Buddhism, which have been widely read and republished. She also founded the Foundation for Traditional Studies, which publishes the journal *Sophia*.

Hakuun Yasutani Roshi (1885–1973) A Soto Zen priest, he became the disciple of Daiun Sogaku Harada Roshi, from whom he received inka in 1943. He founded Sambokyodan, an independent religious organization. Yasutani Roshi made frequent visits to the United States, and in 1970, named Taizan Maezumi as a Dharma successor.

About Wisdom

WISDOM PUBLICATIONS, a nonprofit publisher, is dedicated to making available authentic works relating to Buddhism for the benefit of all. We publish books by ancient and modern masters in all traditions of Buddhism, translations of important texts, and original scholarship. Additionally, we offer books that explore East-West themes unfolding as traditional Buddhism encounters our modern culture in all its aspects. Our titles are published with the appreciation of Buddhism as a living philosophy, and with the special commitment to preserve and transmit important works from Buddhism's many traditions.

To learn more about Wisdom, or to browse books online, visit our website at www.wisdompubs.org.

You may request a copy of our catalog online or by writing to this address:

Wisdom Publications
199 Elm Street
Somerville, Massachusetts 02144 USA
Telephone: 617-776-7416
Fax: 617-776-7841
Email: info@wisdompubs.org
www.wisdompubs.org

THE WISDOM TRUST

As a nonprofit publisher, Wisdom is dedicated to the publication of Dharma books for the benefit of all sentient beings and dependent upon the kindness and generosity of sponsors in order to do so. If you would like to make a donation to Wisdom, you may do so through our website or our Somerville office. If you would like to help sponsor the publication of a book, please write or email us at the address above.

Thank you.

Wisdom is a nonprofit, charitable 501(c)(3) organization affiliated with the Foundation for the Preservation of the Mahayana Tradition (FPMT).